Practical Ethics

William De Witt Hyde

Alpha Editions

This edition published in 2024

ISBN 9789361477065

Design and Setting By

Alpha Editions

www.alphaedis.com

Email - info@alphaedis.com

Contents

PREFACE.   - 1 -

INTRODUCTION.   - 2 -

CHAPTER I.   - 6 -

Food and Drink.   - 6 -

CHAPTER II.   - 11 -

Dress.   - 11 -

CHAPTER III.   - 14 -

Exercise.   - 14 -

CHAPTER IV.   - 18 -

Work.   - 18 -

CHAPTER V.   - 23 -

Property.   - 23 -

CHAPTER VI.   - 27 -

Exchange.   - 27 -

CHAPTER VII.   - 31 -

Knowledge.   - 31 -

CHAPTER VIII.   - 35 -

Time.   - 35 -

CHAPTER IX.   - 38 -

Space.   - 38 -

CHAPTER X.   - 41 -

Fortune.   - 41 -

CHAPTER XI.   - 47 -

Nature.   - 47 -

CHAPTER XII.   - 51 -

Art.   - 51 -

CHAPTER XIII.   - 56 -

Animals.   - 56 -

CHAPTER XIV.   - 60 -

Fellow-men.   - 60 -

CHAPTER XV.   - 67 -

The Poor.   - 67 -

CHAPTER XVI.   - 73 -

Wrongdoers.   - 73 -

CHAPTER XVII.   - 78 -

Friends.   - 78 -

CHAPTER XVIII.   - 82 -

The Family.   - 82 -

CHAPTER XIX.   - 89 -

The State.   - 89 -

CHAPTER XX.   - 94 -

Society.   - 94 -

CHAPTER XXI.   - 101 -

Self.   - 101 -

CHAPTER XXII.   - 109 -

God.   - 109 -

PREFACE.

The steady stream of works on ethics during the last ten years, rising almost to a torrent within the past few months, renders it necessary for even the tiniest rill to justify its slender contribution to the already swollen flood.

On the one hand treatises abound which are exhaustive in their presentation of ethical theory. On the other hand books are plenty which give good moral advice with great elaborateness of detail. Each type of work has its place and function. The one is excellent mental gymnastic for the mature; the other admirable emotional pabulum for the childish mind. Neither, however, is adapted both to satisfy the intellect and quicken the conscience at that critical period when the youth has put away childish things and is reaching out after manly and womanly ideals.

The book which shall meet this want must have theory; yet the theory must not be made obtrusive, nor stated too abstractly. The theory must be deeply imbedded in the structure of the work; and must commend itself, not by metaphysical deduction from first principles, but by its ability to comprehend [iv]in a rational and intelligible order the concrete facts with which conduct has to do.

Such a book must be direct and practical. It must contain clear-cut presentation of duties to be done, virtues to be cultivated, temptations to be overcome, and vices to be shunned: yet this must be done, not by preaching and exhortation, but by showing the place these things occupy in a coherent system of reasoned knowledge.

Such a blending of theory and practice, of faith and works, is the aim and purpose of this book.

The only explicit suggestions of theory are in the introduction (which should not be taken as the first lesson) and in the last two chapters. Religion is presented as the consummation, rather than the foundation of ethics; and the brief sketch of religion in the concluding chapter is confined to those broad outlines which are accepted, with more or less explicitness, by Jew and Christian, Catholic and Protestant, Orthodox and Liberal.

WILLIAM DeWITT HYDE.

BOWDOIN COLLEGE,
BRUNSWICK, ME. May 10, 1892.

INTRODUCTION.

Ethics is the science of conduct, and the art of life.

Life consists in the maintenance of relations; it requires continual adjustment; it implies external objects, as well as internal forces. Conduct must have materials to work with; stuff to build character out of; resistance to overcome; objects to confront.

These objects nature has abundantly provided. They are countless as the sands of the seashore, or the stars of heaven. In order to bring them within the range of scientific treatment we must classify them, and select for study those classes of objects which are most essential to life and conduct. Each chapter of this book presents one of these fundamental objects with which life and conduct are immediately concerned.

A great many different relations are possible between ourselves and each one of these objects. Of these many possible relations some would be injurious to ourselves; some would be destructive of the object. Toward each object there is one relation, and one only, which at the same time best promotes [2]the development of ourselves and best preserves the object's proper use and worth. The maintenance of this ideal union of self and object is our duty with reference to that object.

Which shall come first and count most in determining this right relation, self or object, depends on the character of the object.

In the case of inanimate objects, such as food, drink, dress, and property, the interests of the self are supreme. Toward these things it is our right and duty to be sagaciously and supremely selfish. When persons and mere things meet, persons have absolute right of way.

When we come to ideal objects, such as knowledge, art, Nature, this cool selfishness is out of place. The attempt to cram knowledge, appropriate nature, and "get up" art, defeats itself. These objects have a worth in themselves, and rights of their own which we must respect. They resent our attempts to bring them into subjection to ourselves. We must surrender to them, we must take the attitude of humble and self-forgetful suitors, if we would win the best gifts they have to give, and claim them as our own.

As we rise to personal relations, neither appropriation nor surrender, neither egoism nor altruism, nor indeed any precisely measured mechanical mixture of the two, will solve the problem. Here the recognition of a common good, a commonwealth in which each person has an equal worth with every other, is the only satisfactory solution. "Be a person, and [3]respect the personality of others," is the duty in this sphere.

As we approach social institutions we enter the presence of objects which represent interests vastly wider, deeper, more enduring than the interests of our individual lives. The balance, which was evenly poised when we weighed ourselves against other individuals, now inclines toward the side of these social institutions, without which the individual life would be stripped of all its worth and dignity, apart from which man would be no longer man. Duty here demands devotion and self-sacrifice.

Finally, when we draw near to God, who is the author and sustainer of individuals, of science and art and nature, and of social institutions, then the true relation becomes one of reverence and worship.

In each case duty is the fullest realization of self and object. Whether self or the object shall be the determining factor in the relation depends on whether the object in question has less, equal, or greater worth than the individual self.

If we do our duty repeatedly and perseveringly in any direction, we form the habit of doing it, learn to enjoy it, and acquire a preference for it. This habitual preference for a duty is the virtue corresponding to it.

Virtue is manliness or womanliness. It is the steadfast assertion of what we see to be our duty against the solicitations of temptation. Virtue is mastery; first of self, and through self-mastery, the [4]mastery of the objects with which we come in contact.

Since duty is the maintenance of self and its objects in highest realization, and virtue is constant and joyous fidelity to duty, it follows that duty and virtue cannot fail of that enlargement and enrichment of life which is their appropriate reward.

The reward of virtue will vary according to the duty done and the object toward which it is directed. The virtues which deal with mere things will bring as their rewards material prosperity. The virtues which deal with ideal objects will have their reward in increased capacities, intensified sensibilities, and elevated tastes. The virtues which deal with our fellow-men will be rewarded by enlargement of social sympathy, and deeper tenderness of feeling. The virtues which are directed toward family, state, and society, have their reward in that exalted sense of participation in great and glorious aims, which lift one up above the limitations of his private self, and can make even death sweet and beautiful—a glad and willing offering to that larger social self of which it is the individual's highest privilege to count himself a worthy and honorable member.

Life, however, is not this steady march to victory, with beating drums and flying banners, which, for the sake of continuity in description, we have thus far regarded it. There are hard battles to fight; and mighty foes to conquer. We must now return to those other possible relations which we left when [5]we selected for immediate consideration that one right relation which we call duty.

Since there is only one right relation between self and an object, all others must be wrong. These other possible relations are temptations. Temptation is the appeal of an object to a single side of our nature as against the well-being of self as a whole. Each object gives rise to many temptations. "Broad is the way that leadeth to destruction."

Just as duty performed gives rise to virtue, so temptation, yielded to, begets vice. Vice is the habitual yielding to temptation.

Temptations fall into two classes. Either we are tempted to neglect an object, and so to give it too little influence over us; or else we are tempted to be carried away by an object, and to give it an excessive and disproportionate place in our life. Hence the resulting vices fall into two classes. Vices resulting from the former sort of temptation are vices of defect. Vices resulting from the latter form of temptation are vices of excess. As one of these temptations is usually much stronger than the other, we will discuss simply the strongest and most characteristic temptation in connection with each object. Yet as both classes of vice exist with reference to every object, it will be best to consider both.

Vice carries its penalty in its own nature. Being a perversion of some object, it renders impossible that realization of ourselves through the object, or in the higher relations, that realization of the object [6]through us, on which the harmony and completeness of our life depends. In the words of Plato: "Virtue is the health and beauty and well-being of the soul, and vice is the disease and weakness and deformity of the soul."

Each chapter will follow the order here developed. The outline on pp. vi, vii shows the logical framework on which the book is constructed. Under the limitations of such a table, confined to a single term in every case, it is of course impossible to avoid the appearance of artificiality of form and inadequacy of treatment. This collection of dry bones is offered as the easiest way of exhibiting at a glance the conception of ethics as an organic whole of interrelated members: a conception it would be impossible to present in any other form without entering upon metaphysical inquiries altogether foreign to the practical purpose of the book.

[7]

[8]

[2]

CHAPTER I.

Food and Drink.

The foundations of life, and therefore the first concerns of conduct, are food and drink. Other things are essential if we are to live comfortably and honorably. Food and drink are essential if we are to live at all. In order that we may not neglect these important objects, nature has placed on guard over the body two sentinels, hunger and thirst, to warn us whenever fresh supplies of food and drink are needed.

THE DUTY.

Body and mind to be kept in good working order.—In response to these warnings it is our duty to eat and drink such things, in such quantities, at such times, and in such ways as will render the body the most efficient organ and expression of the mind and will.

Hygiene and physiology, and our own experience and common sense, tell us in detail what, when, and how much it is best for us to eat and drink. Ethics presupposes this knowledge, and simply tells us [10]that these laws of hygiene and physiology are our best friends; and that it is our duty to heed what they say.

THE VIRTUE.

Temperance is self-control.—These sentinels tell us when to begin; but they do not always tell us when to leave off: and if they do, it sometimes requires special effort to heed the warning that they give. The appetite for food and drink, if left to itself, would run away with us. Our liking for what tastes good, if allowed to have its own way, would lead us to eat and drink such things and in such quantities as to weaken our stomachs, enfeeble our muscles, muddle our brains, impair our health, and shorten our lives. Temperance puts bits into the mouth of appetite; holds a tight rein over it; compels it to go, not where it pleases to take us, but where we see that it is best for us to go; and trains it to stop when it has gone far enough.

Virtue means manliness. Temperance is a virtue because it calls into play that strong, firm will which is the most manly thing in us. The temperate man is the strong man. For he is the master, not the slave of his appetites. He is lord of his own life.

THE REWARD.

The temperate man has all his powers perpetually at their best.—Into work or play or study he enters with the energy and zest which come of good digestion, strong muscles, steady nerves, and a [11]clear head. He works hard, plays a strong game, thinks quickly and clearly; because he has a surplus of vitality to throw into whatever he undertakes. He prospers in business because he is able to prosecute it with energy. He makes friends because he has the cheerfulness and vivacity which is the charm of good-fellowship. He enjoys life because all its powers are at his command.

THE TEMPTATION.

The pleasures of taste an incidental good, but not the ultimate good.—Food tastes good to the hungry, and to the thirsty drinking is a keen delight. This is a kind and wise provision of nature; and as long as this pleasure accompanies eating and drinking in a normal and natural way it aids digestion and promotes health and vigor. The more we enjoy our food the better; and food, well-cooked, well-served, and eaten in a happy and congenial company, is vastly better for us than the same food poorly cooked, poorly served, and devoured in solitude and silence.

Yet it is possible to make this pleasure which accompanies eating and drinking the end for the sake of which we eat and drink. The temptation is to eat and drink what we like and as much as we like; instead of what we know to be best for us.

THE VICE OF DEFECT.

The difference between temperance and asceticism.—Asceticism looks like temperance. [12]People who practice it often pride themselves upon it. But it is a hollow sham. And it has done much to bring discredit upon temperance, for which it tries to pass. What then is the difference between temperance and asceticism? Both control appetite. Both are opposed to intemperance. But they differ in the ends at which they aim. Temperance controls appetite for the sake of greater life and health and strength. Asceticism is the control of appetite merely for the sake of controlling it. Asceticism, in shunning the evils to which food and drink may lead, misses also the best blessings they are able to confer. The ascetic attempts to regulate by rule and measure everything he eats and drinks, and to get along with just as little as possible, and so he misses the good cheer and hearty enjoyment which should be the best part of every meal.

Let us be careful not to confound sour, lean, dyspeptic asceticism with the hale, hearty virtue of temperance. Asceticism sacrifices vigor and vitality for the sake of keeping its rules and exercising self-control. Temperance observes the simple rules of hygiene and common sense for the sake of vigor and vitality; and sacrifices the pleasures of the palate only in so far as it is necessary in order to secure in their greatest intensity and permanence the larger and higher interests of life.

Intemperance in eating is gluttony. Intemperance in drinking leads to drunkenness.—Instead of sitting in the seat of reason and driving the appetites before him in obedience to his will, the glutton and the drunkard harness themselves into the wagon and put reins and whip into the hands of their appetites.

The glutton lives to eat; instead of eating to live. This vice is so odious and contemptible that few persons give themselves up entirely to gluttony. Yet every time we eat what we know is not good for us, or more than is good for us, we fall a victim to this loathsome vice.

The drunkard is the slave of an unnatural thirst.—Alcoholic drink produces as its first effect an excitement and exhilaration much more intense than any pleasure coming from the normal gratification of natural appetite. This exhilaration is purchased at the expense of stimulating the system to abnormal exertion. This excessive action of the system during intoxication is followed by a corresponding reaction. The man feels as much worse than usual during the hours and days that follow his debauch, as he felt better than usual during the brief moments that he was taking his drinks. This depression and disturbance of the system which follows indulgence in intoxicating drink begets an unnatural and incessant craving for a repetition of the stimulus; and so in place of the even, steady [14]life of the temperate man, the drinking man's life is a perpetual alternation of brief moments of unnatural excitement, followed by long days of unnatural craving and depression. The habit of indulging this unnatural craving steals upon a man unawares; it occupies more and more of his thought; takes more and more of his time and money, until he is unable to think or care for anything else. It becomes more important to him than business, home, wife, children, reputation, or character; and before he knows it he finds that his will is undermined, reason is dethroned, affection is dead, appetite has become his master, and he has become its beastly and degraded slave.

Total abstinence the only sure defense.—This vice of intemperance is so prevalent in the community, so insidious in its approach, so degrading in its nature, so terrible in its effects, that the only absolutely and universally sure defense against it is total abstinence. A man may think himself strong enough to stop drinking when and where he pleases; but the peculiar and fatal deception about intoxicating drink is that it makes those who become its victims weaker to resist it with every indulgence. It enfeebles their wills directly. The fact that a man can stop drinking to-day is no sure sign that he can drink moderately for a year and stop then. At the end of that time he will have a different body, a different brain, a different mind, a different will from the body and mind and will he has to-day, and would have after a year of abstinence.

[15] As we have seen, with every natural and healthy exercise of our appetites and faculties moderation is preferable to abstinence. It is better to direct them toward the ends they are intended to accomplish that to stifle and suppress them. But the thirst for intoxicating drink is unnatural. It creates abnormal cravings; it produces diseased conditions which corrupt and destroy the very powers of nerve and brain on which the faculties of reason and control depend. "Touch not, taste not, handle not," is the only rule that can insure one against the fearful ravages of this beastly and inhuman vice.

Responsibility for social influence.—A strong argument in favor of abstinence from intoxicating drink is its beneficial social influence. If there are two bridges across a stream, one safe and sure, the other so shaky and treacherous that a large proportion of all who try to cross over it fall into the stream and are drowned; the fact that I happen to have sufficiently cool head and steady nerves to walk over it in safety does not make it right for me to do so, when I know that my companionship and example will lead many to follow who will certainly perish in the attempt.

Mild wines and milder climates may render the moderate use of alcoholic drinks comparatively harmless to races less nervously organized than ours. And there doubtless are individuals in our midst whose strong constitution, phlegmatic temperament, or social training enable them to use wine daily for [16]years without appreciable injury. They can walk with comparative safety the narrow bridge. There are multitudes who cannot. There are tens of thousands for whom our distilled liquors, open saloons, and treating customs, combined with our trying climate and nervous organizations, render moderate drinking practically impossible. They must choose between the safe and sure way of total abstinence, or the fatal plunge into drunkenness and disgrace. And if those who are endowed with cooler heads and stronger nerves are mindful of their social duty to these weaker brethren, among whom are some of the most generous and noble-hearted of our acquaintances and friends, then for the sake of these more sorely tempted ones, and for the sake of their mothers, wives, and sisters to whom a drunken son, husband, or brother is a sorrow worse than death, they will forego a trifling pleasure in order to avert the ruin that their example would otherwise help to bring on the lives, fortunes, and families of others.

Fatal fascination of the opium habit.—What has been said of alcoholic drink is equally true of opium. The habit of using opium is easy to form and almost impossible to break. The secret workings of this poison upon the mind and will of its victim are most insidious and fatal.

Tobacco a serious injury to growing persons.—On this point all teachers are unanimous. Statistics taken at the naval school at Annapolis, at Yale College, and elsewhere, show that the use of [17]tobacco is the exception with scholars at the head, and the rule with scholars at the foot of the class.

Shortly after we began to take statistics on this point in Bowdoin College I asked the director of the gymnasium what was the result with the Freshman class? "Oh," he said, "the list of the smokers is substantially the same as that which was reported the other day for deficiencies in scholarship." A prominent educator, who had given considerable attention to this subject, after spending an hour in my recitation room with a class of college seniors, indicated with perfect accuracy the habitual and excessive smokers, simply by noting the eye, manner, and complexion.

Tobacco, used in early life, tends to stunt the growth, weaken the eyes, shatter the nervous system, and impair the powers of physical endurance and mental application. No candidate for a college athletic team, or contestant in a race, would think of using tobacco while in training. Every man who wishes to keep himself in training for the highest prizes in business and professional life must guard his early years from the deterioration which this habit invariably brings.

THE PENALTY.

These vices bring disease and disgrace.—These vices put in place of physical well-being the gratification of a particular taste and appetite. Hence they bring about the abnormal action of [18]some organs at the expense of all the rest; and this is the essence of disease.

A diseased body causes a disordered mind and an enfeebled will. The excessive and over-stimulated activity of one set of organs involves a corresponding defect in the activity and functions of the other faculties. The glutton or drunkard neglects his business; loses interest in reading and study; fails to provide for his family; forfeits self-respect; and thus brings upon himself poverty and wretchedness and shame. He sinks lower and lower in the social scale; grows more and more a burden to others and a disgrace to himself; and at last ends a worthless and ignominious life in an unwept and dishonored grave.

[19]

CHAPTER II.

Dress.

Next in importance to food and drink stand clothing and shelter. Without substantial and permanent protection against cold and rain, without decent covering for the body and privacy of life, civilization is impossible. The clothes we wear express the standing choices of our will; and as clothes come closer to our bodies than anything else, they stand as the most immediate and obvious expression of our mind. "The apparel oft proclaims the man."

THE DUTY.

Attractive personal appearance.—Clothes that fit, colors that match, cosy houses and cheery rooms cost little more, except in thought and attention, than ill-fitting and unbecoming garments and gloomy and unsightly dwellings. Attractiveness of dress, surroundings, and personal appearance is a duty; because it gives free exercise to our higher and nobler sentiments; elevates and enlarges our lives; while discomfort and repulsiveness in these things lower our standards, and drive us to the baser elements of our nature in search of cheap forms of self-indulgence to take the place of that [20]natural delight in attractive dress and surroundings which has been repressed. Both to ourselves and to our friends we owe as much attractiveness of personal surroundings and personal appearance as a reasonable amount of thought and effort and expenditure can secure.

THE VIRTUE.

Neatness inexpensive and its absence inexcusable.—No one is so poor that he cannot afford to be neat. No one is so rich that he can afford to be slovenly. Neatness is a virtue, or manly quality; because it keeps the things we wear and have about us under our control, and compels them to express our will and purpose.

THE REWARD.

Dress an indication of the worth of the wearer.—Neatness of dress and personal appearance indicates that there is some regard for decency and propriety, some love of order and beauty, some strength of will and purpose inside the garments. If dress is the most superficial aspect of a person, it is at the same time the most obvious one. Our first impression of people is gained from their general appearance, of which dress is one of the most important features.

Consequently dress goes far to determine the estimate people place upon us. Fuller acquaintance may compel a revision of these original impressions. First impressions, however, often decide our fate [21]with people whose respect and good-will is valuable to us. Important positions are often won or lost through attention or neglect in these matters.

THE TEMPTATION.

Dress has its snares.—We are tempted to care, not for attractiveness in itself, but for the satisfaction of thinking, and having others think, how fine we look. Worse still, we are tempted to try to look not as well as we can, but better than somebody else; and by this combination of rivalry with vanity we get the most contemptible and pitiable level to which perversity in dress can bring us. There is no end to the ridiculous and injurious absurdities to which this hollow vanity will lead those who are silly enough to yield to its demands.

Cynicism regarding appearance.—Vanity may take just the opposite form. We may be just as proud of our bad looks, as of our good looks. This is the trick of the Cynic. This is the reason why almost every town has its old codger who seems to delight in wearing the shabbiest coat, and driving the poorest horse, and living in the most dilapidated shanty of anyone in town. These persons take as much pride in their mode of life as the devotee of fashion does in hers. One of these Cynics went to the baths with Alcibiades, the gayest of Athenian youths. When they came out Alcibiades put on the Cynic's rags, leaving his own gay and costly apparel for the Cynic. The Cynic was in a great rage, and [22]protested that he would not be seen wearing such gaudy things as those. "Ah!" said Alcibiades; "so you care more what kind of clothes you wear than I do after all; for I can wear your clothes, but you cannot wear mine." Another of the Cynics, as he entered the elegant apartments of Plato, spat upon the rug, exclaiming: "Thus I pour contempt on the pride of Plato." "Yes," was Plato's reply, "with a greater pride of your own." Since pride and vanity have these two forms, we need to be on our guard against them both. For one or the other is pretty sure to assail us. An eye single to the attractiveness of our personal appearance is the only thing that will save us from one or the other of these lines of temptation.

THE VICE OF DEFECT.

Too little attention to dress and surroundings is slovenliness.—The sloven is known by his dirty hands and face, his disheveled hair, and tattered garments. His house is in confusion; his grounds are littered with rubbish; he eats his meals at an untidy table; and sleeps in an unmade bed. Slovenliness is a vice; for it is an open confession that a man is too weak to make his surroundings the expression of his tastes and wishes, and has allowed his surroundings to run over him and drag him down to their own level. And this subjection of man to the tyranny of things, when he ought to exercise a strong dominion over them, is the universal mark of vice.

[23] THE VICE OF EXCESS.

Too much attention to dress and appearance is fastidiousness.— These things are important; but it is a very petty and empty mind that can find enough in them to occupy any considerable portion of its total attention and energy. The fastidious person must have everything "just so," or the whole happiness of his precious self is utterly ruined. He spends hours upon toilet and wardrobe where sensible people spend minutes. Hence he becomes the slave rather than the master of his dress.

The sloven and the dude are both slaves; but in different ways.— Slovenliness is slavery to the hideous and repulsive. Fastidiousness is slavery to this or that particular style or fashion. The freedom and mastery of neatness consists in the ability to make as attractive as possible just such material as one's means place at his disposal with the amount of time and effort he can reasonably devote to them.

THE PENALTY.

Fastidiousness belittles: slovenliness degrades. Both are contemptible.—The man who does not care enough for himself to keep the dirt off his hands and clothes, when not actually engaged in work that soils them, cannot complain if other people place no higher estimate upon him than he by this slovenliness puts upon himself. The woman whose soul rises and falls the whole distance [24]between ecstasy and despair with the fit of a glove or the shade of a ribbon must not wonder if people rate her as of about equal consequence with gloves and ribbons. These vices make their victims low and petty; and the contempt with which they are regarded is simply the recognition of the pettiness and degradation which the vices have begotten.

[25]

CHAPTER III.

Exercise.

When the body is well fed and clothed, the next demand is for exercise. Our powers are given us to be used; and unless they are used they waste away. Nothing destroys power so surely and completely as disuse. The only way to keep our powers is to keep them in exercise. We acquire the power to lift by lifting; to run, by running; to write, by writing; to talk, by talking; to build houses, by building; to trade, by trading. In mature life our exercise comes to us chiefly along the lines of our business, domestic, and social relations. In childhood and youth, before the pressure of earning a living comes upon us, we must provide for needed exercise in artificial ways. The play-impulse is nature's provision for this need. It is by hearty, vigorous play that we first gain command of those powers on which our future ability to do good work depends.

THE DUTY.

The best exercise that of which we are least conscious.—It is the duty of every grown person as well as of every child to take time for recreation. Exercise taken in a systematic way for its own sake [26]is a great deal better than nothing; and in crowded schools and in sedentary occupations such gymnastic exercises are the best thing that can be had. The best exercise, however, is not that which we get when we aim at it directly; but that which comes incidentally in connection with sport and recreation. A plunge into the river; a climb over the hills; a hunt through the woods; a skate on the pond; a wade in the trout brook; a ride on horseback; a sail on the lake; camping out in the forest;—these are the best ways to take exercise. For in these ways we have such a good time that we do not think about the exercise at all; and we put forth ten times the amount of exertion that we should if we were to stop and think how much exercise we proposed to take.

Next in value to these natural outdoor sports come the artificial games; baseball, football, hare and hounds, lawn tennis, croquet, and hockey. When neither natural nor artificial sports can be had, then the dumb-bells, the Indian clubs, and the foils become a necessity.

Everyone should become proficient in as many of these sports as possible. These are the resources from which the stores of vitality and energy must be supplied in youth, and replenished in later life.

THE VIRTUE.

The value of superfluous energy.—The person whose own life-forces are at their best cannot help flowing over in exuberant gladness to gladden all he [27]meets. Herbert Spencer has set this forth so strongly in his Data of Ethics that I quote his words: "Bounding out of bed after an unbroken sleep, singing or whistling as he dresses, coming down with beaming face ready to laugh at the slightest provocation, the healthy man of high powers enters on the day's business not with repugnance but with gladness; and from hour to hour experiencing satisfaction from work effectually done, comes home with an abundant surplus of energy remaining for hours of relaxation. Full of vivacity, he is ever welcome. For his wife he has smiles and jocose speeches; for his children stories of fun and play; for his friends pleasant talk interspersed with the sallies of wit that come from buoyancy."

THE REWARD.

"Unto everyone that hath shall be given, and he shall have abundance." The reward of exertion is the power to make more exertion the next time. And the reward of habits of regular exercise and habitual cheerfulness is the ability to meet the world at every turn in the consciousness of power to master it, and to meet men with that good cheer which disarms hostility and wins friends.

THE TEMPTATION.

Excitement not to be made an end in itself.—The exhilaration of sport may be carried to the point of excitement; and then this excitement may be made an end in itself. This is the temptation which [28]besets all forms of recreation and amusement. It is the fear of this danger that has led many good people to distrust and disparage certain of the more intense forms of recreation. Their mistake is in supposing that temptation is peculiar to these forms of amusement. As we shall see before we complete our study of ethics, everything brings temptation with it; and the best things bring the severest and subtlest temptations; and if we would withdraw from temptation, we should have to withdraw from the world.

We must all recognize that this temptation to seek excitement for its own sake is a serious one. It is least in the natural outdoor sports like swimming and sailing and hunting and fishing and climbing and riding. Hence we should give to these forms of recreation as large a place as possible in our plans for exercise and amusement. We should see clearly that the artificial indoor amusements, such as dancing, card-playing, theater-going, billiard-playing, are especially liable to give rise to that craving for excitement for excitement's sake which perverts recreation from its true function as a renewer of our powers into a ruinous drain upon them. The moment any form of recreation becomes indispensable to us, the moment we find that it diminishes instead of heightening our interest and delight in the regular duties of our daily lives, that instant we should check its encroachment upon our time and, if need be, cut it off altogether. It is impossible to lay down hard and fast rules, telling precisely [29]what forms of amusement are good and what are bad. So much depends on the attitude of the individual toward them, and the associations which they carry with them in different localities, that what is right and beneficial for one person in one set of surroundings would be wrong and disastrous to another person or to the same person in other circumstances. To enable us to see clearly the important part recreation must play in every healthy life, and to see with equal clearness the danger of giving way to a craving for constant and unnatural excitement, is the most that ethics can do for us. The application of these principles to concrete cases each parent must make for his own children, and each individual for himself.

THE VICE OF DEFECT.

Neglect of exercise and recreation leads to moroseness.—Like milk which is allowed to stand, the spirit of man or woman, if left unoccupied, turns sour. One secret of sourness and moroseness is the sense that some side of our nature has been repressed; and this inward indignation at our own wrongs we vent on others in bitterness and complainings. Moroseness is first a sign that we ourselves are miserable; and secondly it is the occasion of making others miserable too. Having had Spencer's account of the benefits of the cheerfulness that comes from adequate recreation, let us now see his description of its opposite. "Far otherwise is it with one who is enfeebled by great neglect of self. [30]Already deficient, his energies are made more deficient by constant endeavors to execute tasks that prove beyond his strength, and by the resulting discouragement. Hours of leisure, which, rightly passed, bring pleasures that raise the tide of life and renew the powers of work, cannot be utilized: there is not vigor enough for enjoyments involving action, and lack of spirits prevents passive enjoyments from being entered upon with zest. In brief, life becomes a burden. The irritability resulting now from ailments, now from failures caused from feebleness, his family has daily to bear. Lacking adequate energy for joining in them, he has at best but a tepid interest in the amusements of his children; and he is called a wet blanket by his friends."

THE VICE OF EXCESS.

Perpetual amusement-seeking: brings ennui, satiety, and disgust.— "All play and no work makes Jack a mere toy," is as true as that "All work and no play makes Jack a dull boy." The constant pursuit of amusement makes life empty and frivolous. Rightly used recreation increases one's powers for serious pursuits. Pursued wrongly, pursued as the main concern of life, amusement makes all serious work seem stale and dull; and finally makes amusement itself dull and stale too. Ennui, loathing, disgust, and emptiness are the marks of the amusement-seeker the world over. "Vanity of vanities, all is vanity. All things are full of weariness. The eye is not satisfied with seeing nor [31]the ear filled with hearing"—this is the experience of the man who "withheld not his heart from any joy." It is the experience of everyone who exalts amusement from the position of an occasional servant to that of abiding master of his life.

THE PENALTY.

The penalty of neglected exercise is confirmed debility.—"Whosoever hath not, from him shall be taken away even that which he hath." Enfeebled from lack of exercise a man finds himself unequal to the demands of his work; and soured by his consequent dissatisfaction with himself, he becomes alienated from his fellows. The tide of life becomes low and feeble; and he can neither overcome obstacles in his own strength nor attract to himself the help of others.

---

[32]

CHAPTER IV.

Work.

Food, clothes, shelter, and all the necessities of life are the products of labor. Even the simplest food, such as fruit and berries, must be picked before it can be eaten: the coarsest garment of skins must be stripped from the animal before it can be worn: the rudest shelter of rock or cave must be seized and defended against intruders before it can become one's own. And as civilization advances, the element of labor involved in the production of goods steadily increases. The universal necessity of human labor to convert the raw materials given us by nature into articles serviceable to life and enjoyment renders work a fundamental branch of human conduct. Regular meals, comfortable homes, knowledge, civilization, all are the fruits of work. And unless we contribute our part to the production of these goods, we have no moral right to be partakers of the fruits. "If any will not work, neither let him eat." "All work," says Thomas Carlyle, "is noble: work alone is noble. Blessed is he that has found his work; let him ask no other blessedness. Two men I honor, and no third. First, the toilworn craftsman who with [33]earth-made implement laboriously conquers the Earth, and makes her man's. A second man I honor, and still more highly: him who is seen toiling for the spiritually indispensable; not daily bread, but the bread of life. These two in all their degrees I honor; all else is chaff and dust, which let the wind blow whither it listeth. We must all toil, or steal (howsoever we name our stealing), which is worse."

THE DUTY.

Every man lives either upon the fruit of his own work, or upon the fruit of the work of others.—In childhood it is right for us to live upon the fruits of the toil of our parents and friends. But to continue this life of dependence on the work of others after one has become an able-bodied man or woman is to live the life of a perpetual baby. No life so little justifies itself as that of the idle rich. The idle poor man suffers the penalty of idleness in his own person. He gives little to the world; and he gets little in return. The idle rich man gives nothing, and gets much in return. And while he lives, someone has to work the harder for his being in the world; and when he dies the world is left poorer than it would have been had he never been born. He has simply consumed a portion of the savings of his ancestors, and balanced the energy and honor of their lives by his own life of worthlessness and shame. Inherited wealth should bring with it a life of greater responsibility and harder [34]toil; for the rich man is morally bound to use his wealth for the common good. And that is a much harder task than merely to earn one's own living. An able-bodied man who does not contribute to the world at least as much as he takes out of it is a beggar and a thief; whether he shirks the duty of work under the pretext of poverty or riches.

Every boy and girl should be taught some trade, business, art, or profession.—To neglect this duty is to run the risk of enforced dependence upon others, than which nothing can be more destructive of integrity and self-respect. The increasing avenues open to women, and the fact that a woman is liable at any time to have herself and her children to support, make it as important for women as for men to have the ability to earn an honest living.

Woman's sphere is chiefly in the home and the social circle.— Provided she is able to earn her living whenever it becomes necessary, and in case her parents are able and willing to support her, a young woman is justified in remaining in the home until her marriage. Her assistance to her mother in the domestic and social duties of the home, and her preparation for similar duties in her own future home, is often the most valuable service she can render during the years between school and marriage. In order, however, for such a life to be morally justified she must realize that it is her duty to do all in her power to help her mother; to make home more pleasant; and to take part in those forms of social and [35]philanthropic work which only those who have leisure can undertake.

The son or daughter who is to inherit wealth, should be trained in some line of political, scientific, artistic, charitable, or philanthropic work, whereby he may use his wealth and leisure in the service of the public, and justify his existence by rendering to society some equivalent for that security and enjoyment of wealth which society permits him to possess without the trouble of earning it.

All honest work, manual, mental, social, domestic, political and philanthropic, scientific and literary, is honorable. Any form of life without hard work of either hand or brain is shameful and disgraceful. The idler is of necessity a debtor to society; though there are forms of idleness to which, for reasons of its own, society never presents its bill.

THE VIRTUE.

Industry conquers the world.—Industry is a virtue, because it asserts this fundamental interest of self-support in opposition to the solicitations of idleness and ease. Industry masters the world, and makes it man's servant and slave. The industrious man too is master of his own feelings; and compels the weaker and baser impulses of his nature to stand back and give the higher interests room. The industrious man will do thorough work, and produce a good article, cost what it may. He will not suffer his arm to rest until it has done his bidding; nor will he let nature go until her resources and forces [36]have been made to serve his purpose. This mastery over ourselves and over nature is the mark of virtue and manliness always and everywhere.

THE REWARD.

Industry works; and the fruit of work is wealth.—The industrious man may or may not have great riches. That depends on his talents, opportunities, and character. Great riches are neither to be sought nor shunned. With them or without them the highest life is possible; and on the whole it is easier without than with great riches. A moderate amount of wealth, however, is essential to the fullest development of one's powers and the freest enjoyment of life. Of such a moderate competence the industrious man is assured.

THE TEMPTATION.

Soft places and easy kinds of work to be avoided.—Work costs pain and effort. Men naturally love ease. Hence arises the temptation to put ease above self-support. This temptation in its extreme form, if yielded to, makes a man a beggar and a tramp. More frequently the temptation is to take an easy kind of work, rather than harder work; or to do our work shiftlessly rather than thoroughly.

Young men are tempted to take clerkships where they can dress well and do light work, instead of learning a trade which requires a long apprenticeship, and calls for rough, hard work. The result is that the clerk remains a clerk all his life on low wages, [37]and open to the competition of everybody who can read and write and cipher. While the man who has taken time to learn a trade, and has taken off his coat and accustomed himself to good hard work, has an assured livelihood; and only the few who have taken the same time to learn the trade, and are as little afraid of hard work as himself, can compete with him. This temptation to seek a "soft berth," where the only work required is sitting in an office, or talking, or writing, or riding around, is the form of sloth which is taking the strength and independence and manliness out of young men to-day faster than anything else. It is only one degree above the loafer and the tramp. The young man who starts in life by seeking an easy place will never be a success either in business or in character.

THE VICE OF DEFECT.

The slavery of laziness.—Laziness is a vice because it sacrifices the permanent interest of self-support to the temporary inclination to indolence and ease. The lazy man is the slave of his own feelings. His body is his master; not his servant. He is the slave of circumstances. What he does depends not on what he knows it is best to do, but on how he happens to feel. If the work is hard; if it is cold or rainy; if something breaks; or things do not go to suit him, he gives up and leaves the work undone. He is always waiting for something to turn up; and since nothing turns up for our benefit except what we turn up ourselves, he never finds the opportunity [38]that suits him; he fails in whatever he undertakes: and accomplishes nothing. Laziness is weakness, submission, defeat, slavery to feeling and circumstance; and these are the universal characteristics of vice.

THE VICE OF EXCESS.

The folly of overwork.—Work has for its end self-support. Work wisely directed makes leisure possible. Overwork is work for its own sake; work for false and unreal ends; work that exhausts the physical powers. Overwork makes a man a slave to his work, as laziness makes him a slave to his ease. The man who makes haste to be rich; who works from morning until night "on the clean jump"; who drives his business with the fierce determination to get ahead of his competitors at all hazards, misses the quiet joys of life to which the wealth he pursues in such hot haste is merely the means, breaks down in early or middle life, and destroys the physical basis on which both work and enjoyment depend. To undertake more than we can do without excessive wear and tear and without permanent injury to health and strength is wrong. Laziness is the more ignoble vice; but the folly of overwork is equally apparent, and its results are equally disastrous. Laziness is a rot that consumes the base elements of society. Overwork is a tempest that strikes down the bravest and best. That work alone is wrought in virtue which keeps the powers up [39]to their normal and healthful activity, and is subordinated to the end of self-support and harmonious self-development. The ideal attitude toward work is beautifully presented in Matthew Arnold's sonnet on "Quiet Work":

One lesson, Nature, let me learn of thee,One lesson which in every wind is blown;One lesson of two duties kept at oneThough the loud world proclaim their enmity—

Of toil unsevered from tranquillity;Of labor, that in lasting fruit outgrowsFar noisier schemes, accomplished in repose,Too great for haste, too high for rivalry.

THE PENALTY.

Laziness leads to poverty.—The lazy man does nothing to produce wealth. The only way in which he can get it is by inheritance, or by gift, or by theft. Money received by inheritance does not last long. The man who is too lazy to earn money, is generally too weak to use it wisely; and it soon slips through his fingers. When a man's laziness is once found out people refuse to give to him. And the thief cannot steal many times without being caught. Industry is the only sure and permanent title to wealth; and where industry is wanting, there, soon or late, poverty must come.

---

[40]

CHAPTER V.

Property.

The products of labor, saved up and appropriated to our use, constitute property. Without property life cannot rise above the hand-to-mouth existence of the savage. It is as important to save and care for property after we have earned it, as it is to earn it in the first place. Property does not stay with us unless we watch it sharply. Left to itself it takes wings and flies away. Unused land is overgrown by weeds; unoccupied houses crumble and decay; food left exposed sours and molds; unused tools rust; and machinery left to stand idle gets out of order. Everything goes to rack and ruin, unless we take constant care. Hence the preservation of property is one of the fundamental concerns of life and conduct.

THE DUTY.

Provision for family and for old age.—Childhood and old age ought to be free from the necessity of earning a living. Childhood should be devoted to growth and education; old age to enjoyment and repose. In order to secure this provision for old age, for the proper training of children and against sickness and accident, it is a duty to save a portion [41]of one's earnings during the early years of active life. The man who at this period is not doing more than to support himself and family, is not providing for their permanent support at all. They are feasting to-day with the risk of starvation to-morrow.

In primitive conditions of society this provision for the future consisted in the common ownership by family or clan of flocks and herds or lands, whereby the necessities of life were insured to each member of the clan or family from birth to death.

THE VIRTUE.

The importance of systematic saving.—In the more complex civilization of to-day, property assumes ten thousand different forms; is held mostly by individuals; and has for its universal symbol, money. Hence the practical duty is to lay aside a certain sum of money out of our regular earnings each month or week during the entire period of our working life, or from sixteen to sixty. Persons who acquire a liberal education, or learn a difficult trade or profession, will not be able to begin to save until they are twenty or twenty-five. Whenever earning begins, saving should begin. If earnings are small, savings must be small too. He who postpones saving until earnings are large and saving is easy, will postpone saving altogether.

The habit of saving like all habits must be formed early and by conscious and painful effort, or it will not be formed at all. Saving is as much a duty as earning; and the two should begin together. [42]Earning provides for the wants of the individual and the hour. It requires both earning and saving to provide for the needs of a life-time and the welfare of a family. Savings-banks and building and loan associations afford the best opportunities for small savings at regular intervals; and no man has any right to marry until he has a savings-bank account, or shares in a building and loan association, or an equally regular and secure method of systematic saving. In early life, before savings have become sufficient to provide for his family in case of death, it is also a duty to combine saving with life-insurance. Both in investment of savings and in life-insurance, one should make sure that the institution or organization to which he intrusts his money is on a sound business basis. All speculative schemes should be strictly avoided. Any company or form of investment that offers to give back more than you put into it, plus a fair rate of interest on the money, is not a fit place for a man to trust the savings on which the future of himself and his family depends. Security, absolute security, not profits and dividends, is what one should demand of the institution to which he trusts his savings.

Economy eats the apple to the core; wears clothes until they are threadbare; makes things over; gets the entire utility out of a thing; throws nothing away that can be used again; gets its money's worth for every cent expended; buys nothing for which it cannot pay cash down and [43]leave something besides for saving. It is a manly quality, or virtue, because it masters things, keeps them under our control, compels them to render all the service there is in them, and insures our lasting independence.

THE REWARD.

The savings of early and middle life support old age in honorable rest, and give to children a fair start in life.—All men are liable to misfortune and accident. The improvident man is crushed by them; for they find him without reserved force to meet them.

The economical man has in his savings a balance wheel whose momentum carries him by hard places. His position is independent and his prosperity is permanent. For it depends not on the fortunes of the day, which are uncertain and variable; but on the fixed habits and principles of a life-time, which are changeless and reliable.

THE TEMPTATION.

Living beyond one's income: running in debt.—Income is limited; while the things we would like to have are infinite. We must draw the line somewhere. Duty says, draw it well inside of income. Temptation says, draw it at income, or a trifle outside of income. Yield to this temptation, and our earnings are gone before we know it, and debt stares us in the face. Debts are easy to contract, but hard to pay. The debt must be paid [44]sometime with accumulated interest. And when the day of reckoning comes it invariably costs more inconvenience and trouble to pay it than it would have cost to have gone without the thing for the sake of which we ran in debt.

Never, on any account, get in debt. Never spend your whole income. These are rules we are constantly tempted to break. But the man who yields to this temptation is on the high road to financial ruin.

THE VICE OF DEFECT.

Wastefulness.—The wasteful man buys things he does not need; spends his money as fast as he can get it; lives beyond his means; throws things away which are capable of further service; runs in debt; and is forever behindhand. He lives from hand to mouth; is dependent upon his neighbors for things which with a little economy he might own himself; makes no provision for the future, and when sickness or old age comes upon him, he is without resources.

THE VICE OF EXCESS.

Miserliness.—Economy saves for the sake of future expenditure. Miserliness saves for the sake of saving. The spendthrift sacrifices the future to present enjoyment. The miser sacrifices present enjoyment to an imaginary future which never comes; and so misses enjoyment altogether. The prudent man harmonizes present with future enjoyment, and so lives a life of constant enjoyment. [45]The spendthrift spends recklessly, regardless of consequences. The miser hoards anxiously, despising the present. The man of prudence and economy spends liberally for present needs, and saves only as a means to more judicious and lasting expenditure. The miser is as much the slave of his money as is the spendthrift the slave of his indulgences. Economy escapes both forms of slavery and maintains its freedom by making both spending and saving tributary to the true interests of the self.

THE PENALTY.

The thing we waste to-day, we want to-morrow.—The money we spend foolishly to-day we have to borrow to-morrow, and pay with interest the day after. Wastefulness destroys the seeds of which prosperity is the fruit. Wastefulness throws away the pennies, and so must go without the dollars which the pennies make. Years of health and strength spent in hand-to-mouth indulgence inevitably bear fruit in a comfortless old age.

[46]

CHAPTER VI.

Exchange.

The jack-of-all-trades is a bungler in every one of them. The man who will do anything well must confine himself to doing a very few things. Yet while the things a man can produce to advantage are few, the things he wants to consume are many. Exchange makes possible at the same time concentration in production and diversity of enjoyment. Exchange enables the shoemaker to produce shoes, the tailor to make coats, the carpenter to build houses, the farmer to raise grain, the weaver to make cloth, the doctor to heal disease; and at the same time brings to each one of them a pair of shoes, a coat, a house, a barrel of flour, a cut of cloth, and such medical attendance as he needs. Civilization rests on exchange.

THE DUTY.

It is the duty of each party in a trade to give a fair and genuine equivalent for what he expects to receive.—Articles exchanged always represent work. And it is our duty to make sure that the article we offer represents thorough work. Good honest work is the foundation of all righteousness. Whatever we offer for sale, whether it be our [47]labor for wages, or goods for a price, ought to be as good and thorough as we can make it. To sell a day's work for wages, and then to loaf a part of that day, is giving a man idleness when he pays for work. To sell a man a shoddy coat when he thinks he is buying good wool, is giving him cold when he pays for warmth. To give a man defective plumbing in his house when he hires you for a good workman, is to sell him disease and death, and take pay for it. Selling adulterated drugs and groceries is giving a man a stone when he asks for and pays for bread. If, after we have done our best to make or secure good articles, we are unable to avoid defects and imperfections, then it is our duty to tell squarely just what the imperfection is, and sell it for a reduced price. On no other basis than this of making genuine goods, and representing them just as they are, can exchange fulfill its function of mutual advantage to all concerned.

THE VIRTUE.

Honesty looks people straight in the eye, tells the plain truth about its goods, stands on its merits, asks no favors, has nothing to conceal, fears no investigation.—This bold, open, self-reliant quality of honesty is what makes it a manly thing, or a virtue. To do thorough work; to speak the plain truth; to do exactly as you would be done by; to put another man's interest on a level with your own; to take under no pretext or excuse a cent's worth more than you give in any trade you [48]make, calls out all the strength and forbearance and self-control there is in a man, and that is why it ranks so high among the virtues.

THE REWARD.

The honest man is the only man who can respect himself.—He carries his head erect, and no man can put him down. Everything about him is sound and every act will bear examination. This sense of one's own genuineness and worth is honesty's chief reward.

THE TEMPTATION.

Every one-sided transaction dishonest.—In fair exchange both parties are benefited. In unfair exchange one party profits by the other's loss. Any transaction in which either party fails to receive an equivalent for what he gives is a fraud; and the man who knowingly and willfully makes such a trade is a thief in disguise. For taking something which belongs to another, without giving him a return, and without his full, free, and intelligent consent, is stealing.

The temptation to take advantage of another's ignorance; to palm off a poor article for a good one; to get more than we give, is very great in all forms of business. Cheating is very common, and one is tempted to do a little cheating himself in order to keep even with the rest. The only way to resist it is to see clearly that cheating is lying and stealing put together; that it is an injury to our fellow-men [49]and to society; that it is playing the part of a knave and a rascal instead of an honest and honorable man.

THE VICE OF DEFECT.

The meanest and most contemptible kind of cheating is quackery.— The quack is liar, thief, and murderer all in one. For in undertaking to do things for which he has no adequate training and skill, he pretends to be what he is not. He takes money for which he is unable to render a genuine equivalent. And by inducing people to trust their lives in his incompetent and unskilled hands he turns them aside from securing competent treatment, and so confirms disease and hastens death.

The dishonest man a public nuisance and a common enemy.—He gets his living out of other people. Whatever wealth he gets, some honest man who has earned it is compelled to go without. Dishonesty is the perversion of exchange from its noble function as a civilizing agent and a public benefit, into the ignoble service of making one man rich at the expense of the many. It is because the dishonest man is living at other people's expense, profiting by their losses, and fattening himself on the earnings of those whom he has wronged, that dishonesty is deservedly ranked as one of the most despicable and abominable of vices.

THE VICE OF EXCESS.

It is as important to protect our own interest, as to regard the interests of others.—No man [50]has any more right to cheat me than I have to cheat him; and if he tries to take advantage of me it is my duty to resist him, and to say a decided "no" to his schemes for enriching himself at my expense.

One rule in particular is very important. Never sign a note for another in order to give him a credit which he could not command without your name. That is a favor which no man has a right to ask, and which no man who regards his duty to himself and to his family will grant. If a man is in a tight place and asks you to lend him money, or to give him money, that is a proposition to be considered on its merits. But to assume an indefinite responsibility by signing another man's note, is accepting the risk of ruining ourselves for his accommodation. We owe it to ourselves and our families to keep our finances absolutely under our own control, free from all complication with the risks and uncertainties of another's enterprises and fortunes.

Our own rights are as sacred as those of another. There are two sides to every bargain; and one side is as important as the other. The sacrifice of a right may be as great an evil as the perpetration of a wrong.

THE PENALTY.

Dishonesty eats the heart out of a man.—The habit of looking solely to one's own interest deadens the social sympathies, dwarfs the generous affections, weakens self-respect, until at length the dishonest men can rob the widow of her livelihood; take an exorbitant commission on the labor of the [51]orphan; charge an extortionate rent to a family of helpless invalids; sell worthless stocks to an aged couple in exchange for the hard earnings of a life-time, and still endure to live. Dishonesty makes men inhuman. The love of gain is a species of moral and spiritual decay. When it attacks the heart the finer and better feelings wither and die; and on this decay of sympathy and kindness and generosity and justice there thrive and flourish meanness and heartlessness and cruelty and inhumanity.

Hereditary effects of dishonesty.—So deeply does the vice of dishonesty eat into the moral nature that mental and moral deterioration is handed down to offspring. The scientific study of heredity shows that the deterioration resulting from this cause is more sure and fatal than that following many forms of insanity. The son or daughter of a mean, dishonest man is handicapped with tendencies toward moral turpitude and anti-social conduct for which no amount of his ill-gotten gains, received by inheritance, can be an adequate compensation. Says Maudsley, "I cannot but think that the extreme passion for getting rich, absorbing the whole energies of a life, predisposes to mental degeneracy in the offspring, either to moral defect, or to intellectual deficiency, or to outbursts of positive insanity." And the same author says elsewhere: "The anti-social, egoistic development of the individual predisposes to, if it does not predetermine, the mental degeneracy of his progeny; he, alien [52]from his kind by excessive egoisms, determines an alienation of mind in them. If I may trust in that matter my observations, I know no one who is more likely to breed insanity in his offspring than the intensely narrow, self-sensitive, suspicious, distrustful, deceitful, and self-deceiving individual, who never comes into sincere and sound relations with men and things, who is incapable by nature and habit of genuinely healthy communion with himself or with his kind. A moral development of that sort, I believe, is more likely to predetermine insanity in the next generation than are many forms of actual derangement in parents: for the whole moral nature is essentially infected, and that goes deeper down, and is more dangerous, *quâ* heredity, than a particular derangement. A mental alienation is a natural pathological evolution of it."

---

[53]

CHAPTER VII.

Knowledge.

What food is to the body, that knowledge is to the mind. It is the bread of intellectual life. Without knowledge of agriculture and the mechanic arts we should be unable to provide ourselves with food and clothing and houses and ships and roads and bridges. Without knowledge of natural science we should be strangers in the world in which we live, the victims of the grossest superstitions. Without knowledge of history and political science we could have no permanent tranquility and peace, but should pass a precarious existence, exposed to war and violence, rapine and revolution. Knowledge unlocks for us the mysteries of nature; unfolds for us the treasured wisdom of the world's great men; interprets to us the longings and aspirations of our hearts.

Books, we know,Are a substantial world, both pure and good:Round these with tendrils strong as flesh and blood,Our pastime and our happiness will grow.

THE DUTY.

The severity of truth.—Things exist in precise and definite relations. Events take place according [54]to fixed and immutable laws. Truth is the perception of things just as they are. Between truth and falsehood there is no middle ground. Either a fact is so, or it is not. "Truth," says Ruskin, "is the one virtue of which there are no degrees. There are some faults slight in the sight of love, some errors slight in the estimation of wisdom; but truth forgives no insult, and endures no stain." Truth does not always lie upon the surface of things. It requires hard, patient toil to dig down beneath the superficial crust of appearance to the solid rock of fact on which truth rests. To discover and declare truth as it is, and facts as they are, is the vocation of the scholar. Not what he likes to think, not what other people will be pleased to hear, not what will be popular or profitable; but what as the result of careful investigation, painstaking inquiry, prolonged reflection he has learned to be the fact;—this, nothing less and nothing more, the scholar must proclaim. Truth is fidelity to fact; it plants itself upon reality; and hence it speaks with authority. The truthful man is one whom we can depend upon. His word is as good as his bond. "He sweareth to his own hurt, and changeth not." The truthful man brings truth and man together.

THE VIRTUE.

Veracity has two foundations: one reverence for truth; the other regard for one's fellow-men.—Ordinarily these two motives coincide and re-enforce each other. The right of truth to be spoken, and [55]the benefit to men from hearing it, are two sides of the same obligation. Only in the most rare and exceptional cases can these two motives conflict. To a healthy, right-minded man the knowledge of the truth is always a good.

Apparent exceptions to the duty of truthfulness.—We owe truth to all normal people, and under all normal circumstances. We do not necessarily owe it to the abnormal. In sickness, when the patient cannot bear the shock of distressing news; in insanity, when the maniac cannot give to facts their right interpretation; in criminal perversity, when knowledge would be used in furtherance of crime, the abnormal condition of the person with whom we have to deal may justify us in withholding from him facts which he would use to the injury of himself or others. These are very rare and extreme cases, and are apparent rather than real exceptions to the universal rule of absolute truthfulness in human speech. For in these cases it is not from a desire to deceive or mislead the person, that we withhold the truth. We feel sure that the sick person, when he recovers; the insane person when he is restored to reason; the criminal, if he is ever converted to uprightness, will appreciate the kindness of our motive, and thank us for our deed. To the person of sound body, sound mind, and sound moral intent, no conceivable combination of circumstances can ever excuse us from the strict requirement of absolute veracity, or make a lie anything but base, cowardly, and contemptible.

[56] THE REWARD.

Society is founded on trust.—Without confidence in one another, we could not live in social relations a single day. We should relapse into barbarism, strife, and mutual destruction. Since society rests on confidence, and confidence rests on tried veracity, the rewards of veracity are all those mutual advantages which a civilized society confers upon its members.

THE TEMPTATION.

The costliness of strict truthfulness.—Truth is not only hard to discover, but frequently it is costly to speak. Truth is often opposed to sacred traditions, inherited prejudices, popular beliefs, and vested interests. To proclaim truth in the face of these opponents in early times has cost many a man his life; and to-day it often exposes one to calumny and abuse. Hence comes the temptation to conceal our real opinions; to cover up what we know to be true under some phrase which we believe will be popular; to sacrifice our convictions to what we suppose to be our interests.

Especially when we have done wrong the temptation to cover it up with a lie is very great. Deception seems so easy; it promises to smooth over our difficulties so neatly; that it is one of the hardest temptations to resist. Little do we dream,

What a tangled web we weaveWhen first we practice to deceive.

[57] THE VICE OF DEFECT.

The forms of falsehood are numberless.—We may lie by our faces; by our general bearing; by our silence, as well as by our lips. There is "the glistening and softly spoken lie; the amiable fallacy; the patriotic lie of the historian; the provident lie of the politician; the zealous lie of the partisan; the merciful lie of the friend; the careless lie of each man to himself." The mind of man was made for truth: truth is the only atmosphere in which the mind of man can breathe without contamination. No passing benefit which I can secure for myself or others can compensate for the injury which a falsehood inflicts on the mind of him who tells it and on the mind of him to whom it is told. For benefits and advantages, however great and important, are what we have, and they perish with the using. The mind is what we are; and an insult to our intelligence, a scar upon ourselves, a blow at that human confidence which binds us all together, is irremediable.

THE VICE OF EXCESS.

The mischievousness of gossip and scandal.—We are not called upon to know everything that is going on; nor to tell everything that we cannot help knowing. Idle curiosity and mischievous gossip result from the direction of our thirst for knowledge toward trifling and unworthy objects. There is great virtue in minding one's own business. The tell-tale is abhorrent even to the least developed [58]moral sensibility. The gossip, the busybody, the scandalmonger is the worst pest that infests the average town and village. These mischief-makers take a grain of circumstantial evidence, mix with it a bushel of fancies, suspicions, surmises, and inuendoes, and then go from house to house peddling the product for undoubted fact. The scandalmonger is the murderer of reputations, the destroyer of domestic peace, the insuperable obstacle to the mutual friendliness of neighborhoods. This "rejoicing in iniquity" is the besetting sin of idle people. The man or woman who delights in this gratuitous and uncalled-for criticism of neighbors thereby puts himself below the moral level of the ones whose faults he criticises. Martineau, in his scale of the springs of action, rightly ranks censoriousness, with vindictiveness and suspiciousness, at the very bottom of the list. Unless there is some positive good to be gained by bringing wrong to light and offenders to justice we should know as little as possible of the failings of our fellow-men, and keep that little strictly to ourselves.

THE PENALTY.

Falsehood undermines the foundations of social order.—Universal falsehood would bring social chaos. The liar takes advantage of the opportunity which his position as a member of society gives him to strike a deadly blow at the heart of the social order on which he depends for his existence, and without whose aid his arm would be powerless to strike.

[59] **The liar likewise loses confidence in himself.**—He cannot distinguish truth from falsehood, he has so frequently confounded them. He is caught in his own meshes. A good liar must have a long memory. Having no recognized standard to go by, he cannot remember whether he said one thing or another about a given fact; and so he hangs himself by the rope of his own contradictions. Worse than these outward consequences is the loss of confidence in his own integrity and manhood. In Kant's words, "A lie is the abandonment, or, as it were, the annihilation of the dignity of man."

---

[60]

CHAPTER VIII.

Time.

Every act we do, every thought we think, every feeling we cherish exists in time. Our life is a succession of flying moments. Once gone, they can never be recalled. As they are employed, so our character becomes. To use time wisely is a good part of the art of living well, for "time is the stuff life is made of."

THE DUTY.

The duty of making life a consistent whole.—Life is not merely a succession of separate moments. It is an organic whole. The way in which we spend one moment affects the next, and all that follow; just as the condition of one part of the body affects the well-being of all the rest. As we have seen, dissipation to-day means disease to-morrow. Work to-day means property to-morrow. Wastefulness to-day means want to-morrow. Hence it should be our aim so to co-ordinate one period of time with another that our action will promote not merely the immediate interests of the passing moment, but the interests of the permanent self throughout the whole of life. What we pursue on one day must not clash with what we pursue the next; each [61]must contribute its part to our comprehensive and permanent well-being.

THE VIRTUE

Prudence is the habit of looking ahead, and seeing present conduct in its relation to future welfare.—Prudence is manly and virtuous because it controls present inclination, instead of being controlled by it. A burning appetite or passion springs up within us, and demands instant obedience to its demands. The weak man yields at once and lets the appetite or passion or inclination lead him whithersoever it listeth. Not so the strong, the prudent man. He says to the hot, impetuous passion: "Sit down, and be quiet. I will consider your request. If it seems best I will do as you wish. If it turns out that what you ask is not for my interest I shall not do it. You need not think that I am going to do everything you ask me to, whether it is for my interest to do it or not. You have fooled me a good many times, and hereafter I propose to look into the merits of your requests before I grant them." It takes strength and courage and determination to treat the impulses of our nature in this haughty and imperious manner. But the strength and resolution which it takes to do an act is the very essence of its manliness and virtue.

THE REWARD.

The life of the prudent man holds together, part plays into part, and the whole runs smoothly.—One period of life, one fraction of time, [62]does not conflict with another. He looks on the past with satisfaction because he is enjoying the fruit of that past in present well-being. He looks to the future with confidence because the present contains the seeds of future well-being. Each step in life is adjusted to every other, and the result is a happy and harmonious whole.

THE TEMPTATION.

Time tempts us to break up our lives into separate parts.—"Let us eat and drink, for to-morrow we die." "After us the deluge." These are the maxims of fools. The reckless seizure of the pleasures of the present hour, regardless of the days and years to come, is the characteristic mark of folly.

THE VICE OF DEFECT.

"Procrastination is the thief of time."—The particular impulse which most frequently leads us to put off the duty of the hour is indolence. But any appetite or passion which induces us to postpone a recognized duty for the sake of a present delight is an invitation to procrastination.

The fallacy of procrastination, the trick by which it deceives, is in making one believe that at a different time he will be a different person. The procrastinator admits, for instance, that a piece of work must be done. But he argues, "Just now I would rather play or loaf than do the work. By and by there will come a time when I shall rather do the work than play or loaf. Let's wait till that time [63]comes." That time never comes. Our likes and dislikes do not change from one day to another. To-morrow finds us as lazy as to-day, and with the habit of procrastination strengthened by the indulgence of yesterday. Putting a duty off once does not make it easier: it makes it harder to do the next time.

Play or rest when we ought to be at work is weakening and demoralizing. Rest and play after work is bracing and invigorating. The sooner we face and conquer a difficulty, the less of a difficulty it is. The longer we put it off the greater it seems, and the less becomes our strength with which to overcome it.

THE VICE OF EXCESS.

Anxiety defeats itself.—Anxiety sacrifices the present to the future. When this becomes a habit it defeats its own end. For the future is nothing but a succession of moments, which, when they are realized, are present moments. And the man who sacrifices all the present moments to his conception of a future, sacrifices the very substance out of which the real future is composed. For when he reaches the time to which he has been looking forward, and for the sake of which he has sacrificed all his early days, the habit of anxiety stays by him and compels him to sacrifice that future, now become present, to another future, still farther ahead; and so on forever. Thus life becomes an endless round of fret and worry, full of imaginary ills, [64]destitute of all real and present satisfaction. It is a good rule never to cross a bridge until we come to it. Prudence demands that we make reasonable preparation for crossing it in advance. But when these preparations are made prudence has done its work, and waits calmly until the time comes to put its plans into operation. Anxiety fills all the intervening time with forebodings of all the possible obstacles that may arise when the time for action comes.

Procrastination, anxiety, and prudence.—Procrastination sacrifices the future to the present. Anxiety sacrifices the present to the future. Prudence co-ordinates present and future in a consistent whole, in which both present and future have their proper place and due consideration.

THE PENALTY.

Imperfect co-ordination, whether by procrastination or by worry, brings discord. The parts of life are at variance with each other. The procrastinator looks on past indulgence with remorse and disgust; for that past indulgence is now loading him down with present disabilities and pains. He looks on the future with apprehension, for he knows that his present pleasures are purchased at the cost of misery and degradation in years to come.

The man in whom worry and anxiety have become habitual likewise lives a discordant life. He looks out of a joyless present, back on a past devoid of interest, and forward into a future full of fears.

[65]

CHAPTER IX.

Space.

As all thoughts and actions take place in time, so all material things exist in space. Everything we have must be in some place. To give things their right relations in space is one of the important aspects of conduct.

THE DUTY.

A place for everything, and everything in its place.—Things that belong together should be kept together. Dishes belong in the cupboard; clothes in the closet; boxes on the shelves; loose papers in the waste basket; tools in the tool-chest; wood in the wood-shed. And it is our duty to keep them in their proper place, when not in actual use. In business it is of the utmost importance to have a precise place for everything connected with it. The carpenter or machinist must have a place for each tool, and always put it there when he is through using it. The merchant must have a definite book and page or drawer or pigeon-hole for every item which he records. The scholar must have a set of cards or envelopes or drawers or pockets alphabetically arranged in which he keeps each class of facts where he can turn to it instantly. This keeping things of a kind together, each kind in a place by itself, is [66]system. Without system nothing can be managed well, and no great enterprise can be carried on at all.

THE VIRTUE.

Orderliness is manly and virtuous because it keeps things under our own control, and makes them the expression of our will.—The orderly and systematic man can manage a thousand details with more ease and power than a man without order and system can manage a dozen. It is not power to do more work than other men, but power to do the same amount of work in such an orderly and systematic way that it accomplishes a hundred times as much as other men's work, which marks the difference between the statesman who manages the affairs of a nation or the merchant prince who handles millions of dollars, and the man of merely ordinary administrative and business ability.

THE REWARD.

The orderly man has his resources at his disposal at a moment's notice.—He can go directly to the thing he wants and be sure of finding it in its place. When a business is thoroughly systematized it is as easy to find one thing out of ten thousand as it is to find one thing out of ten. Hence there is scarcely any limit to the expansion of business of which the systematic man is capable. A business thus reduced to system will almost run itself. Thus the heads of great concerns are able to accept public office, or to spend a year in Europe, [67]in absolute confidence that the business will be well conducted in their absence, and that they can take it up when they return just as they left it. For they know that each man has his part of the work for which he is responsible; each process has its precise method by which it is to be performed; each account has its exact place where it is to be kept. Order and system are the keys to business success. Orderliness keeps things under our control, and the convenience and efficiency with which things serve us is the direct and necessary consequence of having them under control.

THE TEMPTATION.

System takes more labor to begin with, but in the long run system is the greatest labor-saving device in the world.—It takes ten times as long to hunt up a thing which we have left lying around the next time we want it, as it does to put it where it belongs at first. Yet, well as we know this fact, present and temporary ease seems of more consequence at the time of action than future and permanent convenience. Until by repeated exercise and painful discipline we make orderliness and system habitual and almost instinctive, the temptation to make the quickest and handiest disposition of things for which we have no immediate use will continue to beset our minds and betray our wills.

THE VICE OF DEFECT.

The careless man lets things run over him.—They mock him, and make fun of him; getting [68]in his way and tripping him up at one time; hiding from him and making him hunt after them at another. Carelessness is a confession of a weak will that cannot keep things under control. And weakness is ever the mark of vice.

THE VICE OF EXCESS.

The end and aim of system is to expedite business. Red tape is the idolatry of system. It is system for the sake of system.—Every rule admits exceptions. To make exceptions before a habit is fully formed is dangerous; and while we are learning the habit of orderliness and system we should put ourselves to very great inconvenience rather than admit an exception to our systematic and orderly way of doing things. When, however, the habit has become fixed, it is wise and right to sacrifice order and system, when some "short cut" will attain our end more quickly and effectively than the regular and more round-about way of orderly procedure. The strong and successful business man is he who has his system so thoroughly under his control that he can use it or dispense with it on a given occasion; according as it will further or hinder the end he has in view.

THE PENALTY.

The careless man is always bothered by things he does not want getting in his way; and by things that he does want keeping out of his way.—Half his time is spent in clearing away [69]accumulated obstructions and hunting after the things he needs. Where everything is in a heap it is necessary to haul over a dozen things in order to find the one you are after. Carelessness suffers things to get the mastery over us; and the consequence is that we and our business are ever at their mercy. And as things held in control are faithful and efficient servants, so things permitted to domineer over us and do as they please become cruel and arbitrary masters. They waste our time, try our patience, destroy our business, and scatter our fortunes.

---

[70]

CHAPTER X.

Fortune.

Strictly speaking, there is no such thing as fortune, chance, or accident. All things are held together by invariable laws. Every event takes place in accordance with law. Uniformity of law is the condition and presupposition of all our thinking. The very idea of an event that has no cause is a contradiction in terms to which no reality can correspond, like the notion of two mountains without a valley between; or a yard stick with only one end.

Relatively to us, and in consequence of the limitation of our knowledge, an event is a result of chance or fortune when the cause which produced it lies beyond the range of our knowledge. What we cannot anticipate beforehand and what we cannot account for afterward, we group together into a class and ascribe to the fictitious goddess Fortune; as children attribute gifts at Christmas which come from unknown sources to Santa Claus. In reality these unexplained and unanticipated events come from heredity, environment, social institutions, the forces of nature, and ultimately from God.

These things which project themselves without warning into our lives, often have most momentous [71]influence for good or evil over us; and the proper attitude to take toward this class of objects is worthy of consideration by itself.

THE DUTY.

The secret of superiority to fortune.—Some things are under our control; others are not. It is the part of wisdom to concentrate our thought and feeling on the former; working with utmost diligence to make the best use of those things which are committed to us in the regular line of daily duty, and treating with comparative indifference those things which affect us from without. What we are; what we do; what we strive for;—these are the really important matters; and these are always in our power. What money comes to us; what people say about us; what positions we are called to fill; to what parties we are invited; to what offices we are elected, are matters which concern to some extent our happiness. We should welcome these good things when they come. But they affect the accidents rather than the substance of our lives. We should not be too much bound up in them when they come; and we should not grieve too deeply when they go. We should never stake our well-being and our peace of mind on their presence or their absence. We should remember that "The aids to noble life are all within."

This lesson of superiority to fortune, by regarding the things she has to give as comparatively indifferent, is the great lesson of Stoicism. Marcus [72]Aurelius, Epictetus, and Seneca are the masters of this school. Their lesson is one we all need to learn thoroughly. It is the secret of strength to endure the ills of life with serenity and fortitude. And yet it is by no means a complete account of our duty toward these outward things. It is closely akin to pride and self-sufficiency. It gives strength but not sweetness to life. One must be able to do without the good things of fortune if need be. The really strong man, however, is he who can use and enjoy them without being made dependent on them or being enslaved by them. The real mastery of fortune consists not in doing without the things she brings for fear they will corrupt and enslave us; but in compelling her to give us all the things we can, and then refusing to bow down to her in hope of getting more. This just appreciation of fortune's gifts is doubtless hard to combine with perfect independence. The Stoic solution of the problem is easier. The really strong man, however, is he who

Gathers earth's whole good into his arms;Marching to fortune, not surprised by her,

and the secret of this conquest of fortune without being captivated by her lies in having, as Browning telling us,

One great aim, like a guiding star above,Which tasks strength, wisdom, stateliness, to liftHis manhood to the height that takes the prize.

The shortcoming of the Stoics is not in the [73]superiority to fortune which they seek; but in the fact that they seek it directly by sheer effort of naked will, instead of being lifted above subjection to fortune by the attractive power of generous aims, and high ideals of social service.

THE VIRTUE.

The virtue which maintains superiority over external things and forces is courage.—In primitive times the chief form of fortune was physical danger, and superiority to fear of physical injury was the original meaning of courage. Courage involves this physical bravery still; but it has come to include a great deal more. In a civilized community, physical danger is comparatively rare. Courage to do right when everyone around us is doing wrong; courage to say "No" when everyone is trying to make us say "Yes"; courage to bear uncomplainingly the inevitable ills of life;—these are the forms of courage most frequently demanded and most difficult to exercise in the peaceful security of a civilized community. This courage which presents an unruffled front to trouble, and bears bravely the steady pressure of untoward circumstance, we call by the special names of fortitude or patience. Patience and fortitude are courage exercised in the conditions of modern life. The essence of courage is superiority to outside forces and influences. When men were beset by lions and tigers, by Indians and hostile armies, then courage showed itself by facing and fighting these enemies. Now [74]that we live with civilized and friendly men and women like ourselves, courage shows itself chiefly by refusing to surrender our convictions of what is true and right just because other people will like us better if we pretend to think as they do; and by enduring without flinching the rubs and bumps and bruises which this close contact with our fellows brings to us.

Moral courage.—The brave man everywhere is the man who has a firm purpose in his own breast, and goes forth to carry out that purpose in spite of all opposition, or solicitation, or influence of any kind that would tend to make him do otherwise. He does the same, whether men blame or approve; whether it bring him pain or pleasure, profit or loss. The purpose that is in him, that he declares, that he maintains, that he lives to realize; in defense of that he will lay down wealth, reputation, and, if need be, life itself. He will be himself, if he is to live at all. Men must approve what he really is, or he will have none of their praise, but their blame rather. By no pretense of being what he is not, by no betrayal of what he holds to be true and right, will he gain their favor. The power to stand alone with truth and right against the world is the test of moral courage. The brave man plants himself on the eternal foundations of truth and justice, and bids defiance to all the forces that would drive him from it.

Wordsworth, in his character of "The Happy Warrior," has portrayed the kind of courage demanded of the modern man:

[75]'Tis he whose law is reason; who dependsUpon that law as on the best of friends.Who if he rise to station of commandRises by open means, and there will standOn honorable terms, or else retire,And in himself possess his own desire:Who comprehends his trust, and to the sameKeeps faithful with a singleness of aim;And therefore does not stoop nor lie in waitFor wealth, or honors, or for worldly state;Whom they must follow, on whose head must fallLike showers of manna, if they come at all.'Tis finally the man, who, lifted high,Conspicuous object in a nation's eye,Or left unthought of in obscurity,Who with a toward or untoward lot,Prosperous or adverse, to his wish or not,Plays in the many games of life, that oneWhere what he most doth value must be won:Whom neither shape of danger can dismay,Nor thought of tender happiness betray;Who, not

content that former worth stand fast,Looks forward, persevering to the last,From well to better, daily self-surpast:This is the happy warrior; this is heThat every man in arms should wish to be.

THE REWARD.

Courage universally honored.—There is something in this strong, steady power of self-assertion that compels the admiration of everyone who beholds it. When we see a man standing squarely on his own feet; speaking plainly the thoughts that are in his mind; doing fearlessly what he believes to be right; or no matter how widely we may differ from his views, [76]disapprove his deeds, we cannot withhold our honor from the man himself. No man was ever held in veneration by his countrymen; no man ever handed down to history an undying fame, who did not have the courage to speak and act his real thought and purpose in defiance of the revilings and persecutions of his fellows.

THE TEMPTATION.

To take one's fortune into his own hands and work out, in spite of opposition and misfortune, a satisfactory career tasks strength and resolution to the utmost.—It is so much more easy to give over the determination of our fate to some outside power that the abject surrender to fortune is a serious temptation. Air-castles and day-dreams, and idle waiting for something to turn up, are the feeble forms of this temptation. The impulse to run away from danger, and the impulse to plunge recklessly into risks, are the two forms of temptation which lead to the more pronounced and prevalent vices.

THE VICE OF DEFECT.

Yielding to outward pressure, contrary to our own conviction of what is true and right, is moral cowardice.—In early times the coward was the man who turned his back in battle. To-day the coward is the man who does differently when people are looking at him from what he would do if he were alone; the man who speaks what he thinks people want to hear, instead of what he [77]knows to be true; the man who apes other people for fear they will think him odd if he acts like himself; the man who tries so hard to suit everybody that he has no mind of his own; the man who thinks how things will look, instead of thinking how things really are. Whenever we take the determination of our course of conduct ultimately from any other source than our own firm conviction of what is right and true, then we play the coward. We do in the peaceful conditions of modern life just what we despise a soldier for doing on the field of battle. We acknowledge that there is something outside us that is stronger than we are; of which we are afraid; to which we surrender ourselves as base and abject slaves.

THE VICE OF EXCESS.

There are forces in the world that can destroy us; we must protect ourselves against them.—To be truly brave, we must be ready to face these forces when there is a reason for so doing. We must be ready to face the cannon for our country; to plunge into the swollen stream to save the drowning child; to expose ourselves to contagious diseases in order to nurse the sick.

To do these things without sufficient reason is foolhardiness. To expose ourselves needlessly to disease; to put ourselves in the range of a cannon, to jump into the stream, with no worthy end in view, or for the very shallow reason of showing off how brave we can be, is folly and madness. Doing [78]such things because someone dares us to do them is not courage, but cowardice.

Gambling, the most fatal form of this fondness for taking needless risks.—The gambler is too feeble in will, too empty in mind, too indolent in body to carve out his destiny with his own right hand. And so he stakes his well-being on the throw of the dice; the turn of a wheel; or the speed of a horse. This invocation of fortune is a confession of the man's incompetence and inability to solve the problem of his life satisfactorily by his own exertions. It is the most demoralizing of practices. For it establishes the habit of staking well-being not on one's own honest efforts, but on outside influences and forces. It is the dethronement of will and the deposition of manhood.

In addition to being degrading to the individual it is injurious to others. It is anti-social. It makes one man's gain depend on another's loss: while the social welfare demands that gains shall in all cases be mutual. It violates the fundamental law of equivalence.

Since the essence of gambling is the abrogation of the will, every indulgence weakens the power to resist the temptation. Gambling soon becomes a mania. Honest ways of earning money seem slow and dull. And the habit becomes confirmed before the victim is aware of the power over him that it has gained. Every form of gain which is contingent upon another's loss partakes of the nature of gambling. Raffling, playing for stakes, betting, buying [79]lottery tickets, speculation in which there is no real transfer of goods, but mere winning or losing on the fluctuations of the market, are all forms of gambling. They are all animated by the desire to get something for nothing: a desire which we can respect when a helpless pauper asks for alms; but of which in any form an able-bodied man ought to be ashamed.

THE PENALTY.

The shame of cowardice.—Man is meant to be superior to things outside him. When we see him bowing down to somebody whom he does not really believe in; when we see him yielding to forces which he does not himself respect; when living is more to him than living well; when there is a threat which can make him cringe, or a bribe that can make his tongue speak false—then we feel that the manhood has gone out of him, and we cannot help looking on his fall with sorrow and with shame. The penalty which follows moral cowardice is nowhere more clearly stated than in these severe and solemn lines which Whittier wrote when he thought a great man had sacrificed his convictions to his desire for office and love of popularity:

So fallen! so lost! the light withdrawnWhich once he wore!The glory from his gray hairs goneForevermore!

Of all we loved and honored, naughtSave power remains,—[80] A fallen angel's pride of thought,Still strong in chains.

All else is gone, from those great eyesThe soul has fled:When faith is lost, when honor dies,The man is dead!

Then pay the reverence of old daysTo his dead fame;Walk backward, with averted gaze,And hide the shame.

------

[81]

CHAPTER XI.

Nature.

Thus far we have been considering the uses to which we may put the particular things which nature places at our disposal. In addition to these special uses of particular objects, Nature has a meaning as a whole. The Infinite Reason in whose image our minds are formed and in whose thought our thinking, so far as it is true, partakes, has expressed something of his wisdom, truth, and beauty, in the forms and laws of the world in which we live. In the study of Nature we are thinking God's thoughts after him. In contemplation of the glory of the heavens, in admiration of the beauty of field and stream and forest, we are beholding a loveliness which it was his delight to create, and which it is elevating and ennobling for us to look upon. Nature is the larger, fairer, fuller expression of that same intelligence and love which wells up in the form of consciousness within our own breasts. Nature and the soul of man are children of the same Father. Nature is the interpretation of the longings of our hearts. Hence when we are alone with Nature in the woods and fields, by the seashore or on the moon-lit lake, we feel at peace with ourselves, and at home in the world.

[82] THE DUTY.

The love of nature, like all love, cannot be forced.—It is not directly under the control of our will. We cannot set about it in deliberate fashion, as we set about earning a living. Still it can be cultivated. We can place ourselves in contact with Nature's more impressive aspects. We can go away by ourselves; stroll through the woods, watch the clouds; bask in the sunshine; brave the storm; listen to the notes of birds; find out the haunts of living creatures; learn the times and places in which to find the flowers; gaze upon the glowing sunset, and look up into the starry skies. If we thus keep close to Nature, she will draw us to herself, and whisper to us more and more of her hidden meaning.

The eye—it cannot choose but see;We cannot bid the year be still:Our bodies feel, where'er they be,Against or with our will.

Nor less I deem that there are powersWhich of themselves our minds impress;That we can feed these minds of oursIn a wise passiveness.

THE VIRTUE.

- 47 -

The more we feel of the beauty and significance of Nature the more we become capable of feeling.—And this capacity to feel the influences which Nature is constantly throwing around us is an indispensable element in noble and elevated [83]character. Our thoughts, our acts, yes, our very forms and features reflect the objects which we habitually welcome to our minds and hearts. And if we will have these expressions of ourselves noble and pure, we must drink constantly and deeply at Nature's fountains of beauty and truth. Wordsworth, the greatest interpreter of Nature, thus describes the effect of Nature's influence upon a sensitive soul:

She shall be sportive as the fawnThat wild with glee across the lawnOr up the mountain springs;And hers shall be the breathing balm,And hers the silence and the calmOf mute, insensate things.

The floating clouds their state shall lendTo her; for her the willow bend:Nor shall she fail to see,Even in the motions of the storm,Grace that shall mold the maiden's formBy silent sympathy.

The stars of midnight shall be dearTo her; and she shall lean her earIn many a secret placeWhere rivulets dance their wayward round,And Beauty born of murmuring soundShall pass into her face.

THE REWARD.

The uplifting and purifying power of nature.—Through communion with the grandeur and majesty [84]of Nature, our lives are lifted to loftier and purer heights than our unaided wills could ever gain. We grow into the likeness of that we love. We are transformed into the image of that which we contemplate and adore. We are thus made strong to resist the base temptations; patient to endure the petty vexations; brave to oppose the brutal injustices, of daily life. This whole subject of the power of Nature to uplift and bless has been so exhaustively and beautifully expressed by Wordsworth, that fidelity to the subject makes continued quotation necessary:

Nature never did betrayThe heart that loved her; 'tis her privilege,Through all the years of this our life, to leadFrom joy to joy: for she can so informThe mind that is within us, so impressWith quietness and beauty, and so feedWith lofty thoughts, that neither evil tongues,Rash judgments, nor the sneers of selfish men,Nor greetings where no kindness is, nor allThe dreary intercourse of daily life,Shall e'er prevail against us, or disturbOur cheerful faith, that all which we beholdIs full of blessings.

Therefore am I stillA lover of the meadows and the woodsAnd mountains; and of all that we beholdFrom this green earth; well pleased to recognizeIn Nature and the language of the senseThe anchor of my purest thoughts, the nurse,The guide, the guardian of my heart, and soulOf all my moral being.

[85] THE TEMPTATION.

The very thoroughness and fidelity with which we fulfill one duty, may hinder the fulfillment of another.—We may become so absorbed in earning a living, and carrying on our business, and getting an education, that we shall give no time or attention to this communion with Nature. The fact that business, education, and kindred external and definite pursuits are directly under the control of our wills, while this power to appreciate Nature is a slow and gradual growth, only indirectly under our control, tempts us to give all our time and strength to these immediate, practical ends, and to neglect that closer walk with Nature which is essential to a true appreciation of her loveliness. Someone asks us "What is the use of spending your time with the birds among the trees, or on the hill-top under the stars?" and we cannot give him an answer in dollars and cents. And so we are tempted to take his simple standard of utility in ministering to physical wants as the standard of all worth. We neglect Nature, and she hides her face from our preoccupied eyes. In this busy, restless age we need to keep ever in mind Wordsworth's warning against this fatal temptation:

The world is too much with us; late and soon,Getting and spending, we lay waste our powers:Little we see in Nature that is ours;We have given our hearts away, a sordid boon!

[86] THE VICE OF DEFECT.

This obtuseness does not come upon us suddenly. All children keenly appreciate the changing moods of Nature. It is from neglect to open our hearts to Nature, that obtuseness comes. It steals over us imperceptibly. We can correct it only by giving ourselves more closely and constantly to Nature, and trusting her to win back to herself our benumbed and alienated hearts.

THE VICE OF EXCESS.

Affectation the attempt to work up by our own efforts an enthusiasm for Nature.—True love of Nature must be born within us, by the working of Nature herself upon our hearts. By faith, rather than by works; by reception, rather than by conquest; by wise passiveness, rather than by restless haste; by calm and silence, rather than by noise and talk, our sensitiveness to Nature's charms is deepened and developed. That enjoyment of Nature which comes spontaneously and unsought is the only true enjoyment. That which we work up, and plan for, and talk about, is a poor and feeble imitation. The real lover of Nature is not the one who can talk glibly about her to everybody, and on all occasions. It is he who loves to be alone with her, who steals away from men and things to find solitude with her the best society, who knows not whence cometh nor [87]whither goeth his delight in her companionship, who waits patiently in her presence, and is content whether she gives or withholds her special favors, who cares more for Nature herself than for this or that striking sensation she may arouse. Affectation is the craving for sensations regardless of their source. And if Nature is chary of striking scenes and startling impressions and thrilling experiences, affectation, with profane haste, proceeds to amuse itself with artificial feelings, and pretended raptures. This counterfeited appreciation, like all counterfeits, by its greater cheapness drives out the real enjoyment; and the person who indulges in affectation soon finds the power of genuine appreciation entirely gone. Affectation is worse than obtuseness, for obtuseness is at least honest: it may mend its ways. But affectation is self-deception. The affected person does not know what true appreciation of Nature is: he cannot see his error; and consequently cannot correct it.

THE PENALTY.

The life of man can be no deeper and richer than the objects and thoughts on which it feeds.—Without appreciation and love for Nature we can eat and drink and sleep and do our work. The horse and ox, however, can do as much. Obtuseness to the beauty and meaning of Nature sinks us to the level of the brutes. Cut off from the springs of inspiration, our lives stagnate, our souls shrivel, our sensibilities wither. And just as stagnant [88]water soon becomes impure, and swarms with low forms of vegetable and animal life, so the stagnant soul, which refuses to reflect the beauty of sun and star and sky, soon becomes polluted with sordidness and selfishness and sensuality.

[89]

CHAPTER XII.

Art.

Nature is incomplete. She leaves man to provide for himself his raiment, shelter, and surroundings. Nature in her works throws out suggestions of beauty, rather than its perfect and complete embodiment. Her gold is imbedded in the rock. Her creations are limited by the particular material and the narrow conditions which are at her disposal at a given time and place. To seize the pure ideal of beauty which Nature suggests, but never quite realizes; to select from the universe of space and the eternity of time those materials and forms which are perfectly adapted to portray the ideal beauty; to clothe the abodes and the whole physical environment of man with that beauty which is suggested to us in sky and stream and field and flower; to present to us for perpetual contemplation the form and features of ideal manhood and womanhood; to hold before our imagination the deeds of brave men, and the devotion of saintly women; to thrill our hearts with the victorious struggle of the hero and the death-defying passion of the lover;—this is the mission and the significance of art.

Art is creative. The artist is a co-worker with [90]God. To his hands is committed the portion of the world which God has left unfinished—the immediate environment of man. We cannot live in the fields, like beasts and savages. Art has for its purpose to make the rooms and houses and halls and streets and cities in which civilized men pass their days as beautiful and fair, as elevating and inspiring, as the fields and forests in which the primeval savage roamed. More than that, art aims to fill these rooms and halls and streets of ours with forms and symbols which shall preserve, for our perpetual admiration and inspiration, all that is purest and noblest and sweetest in that long struggle of man up from his savage to his civilized estate.

THE DUTY.

Beauty is the outward and visible sign of inward perfection, completeness, and harmony.—In an object of beauty there is neither too little nor too much; nothing is out of place; nothing is without its contribution to the perfect whole. Each part is at once means and end to every other. Hence its perfect symmetry; its regular proportions; its strict conformity to law.

The mind of man can find rest and satisfaction in nothing short of perfection; and consequently our hearts are never satisfied until they behold beauty, which is perfection's crown and seal. Without it one of the deepest and divinest powers of our nature remains dwarfed, stifled, and repressed.

[91] **How to cultivate the love of beauty.**—It is our duty to see to it that everything under our control is as beautiful as we can make it. The rooms we live in; the desk at which we work; the clothes we wear; the house we build; the pictures on our walls; the garden and grounds in which we walk and work; all must have some form or other. That form must be either beautiful or hideous; attractive or repulsive. It is our duty to pay attention to these things; to spend thought and labor, and such money as we can afford upon them, in order to make them minister to our delight. Not in staring at great works of art which we have not yet learned to appreciate, but by attention to the beauty or ugliness of the familiar objects that we have about us and dwell with from day to day, we shall best cultivate that love of beauty which will ultimately make intelligible to us the true significance of the masterpieces of art. Here as everywhere, to him that hath shall more be given. We must serve beauty humbly and faithfully in the little things of daily life, if we will enjoy her treasures in the great galleries of the world.

THE VIRTUE.

Beauty is a jealous mistress.—If we trifle with her; if we fall in love with pretentious imitations and elaborate ornamentations which have no beauty in them, but are simply gotten up to sell; then the true and real beauty will never again suffer us to see her face. She will leave us to our idols: and [92]our power to appreciate and admire true beauty will die out.

Fidelity to beauty requires that we have no more things than we can either use in our work, or enjoy in our rest. And these things that we do have must be either perfectly plain; or else the ornamentation about them must be something that expresses a genuine admiration and affection of our hearts. A farmer's kitchen is generally a much more attractive place than his parlor; just because this law of simplicity is perfectly expressed in the one, and flagrantly violated in the other. The study of a scholar, the office of the lawyer and the business man, is not infrequently a more beautiful place, one in which a man feels more at home, than his costly drawing room. What sort of things we shall have, and how many, cannot be determined for us by any general rule; still less by aping somebody else. In our housekeeping, as in everything else, we should begin with the few things that are absolutely essential; and then add decoration and ornament only so fast as we can find the means of gratifying cherished longings for forms of beauty which we have learned to admire and love. "Simplicity of life," says William Morris, "even the barest, is not a misery, but the very foundation of refinement: a sanded floor and whitewashed walls, and the green trees, and flowery meads, and living waters outside. If you cannot learn to love real art, at least learn to hate sham art and reject it. If the real thing is not to be had, learn to do without it. If you want a [93]golden rule that will fit everybody, this is it: Have nothing in your houses that you do not know to be useful, or believe to be beautiful."

THE REWARD.

The refining influence of beauty.—Devotion to art and beauty in simplicity and sincerity develops an ever increasing capacity for its enjoyment. As Keats, the master poet of pure beauty, tells us,

A thing of beauty is a joy forever:Its loveliness increases; it will neverPass into nothingness; but still will keepA bower quiet for us, and a sleep,Full of sweet dreams, and health, and quiet breathing.

The refining influence of the love of beauty draws us mysteriously and imperceptibly, but none the less powerfully, away from what is false in thought and base in action; and develops a deep and lasting affinity for all that is true and good. The good, the true, and the beautiful are branches of a common root; members of a single whole: and if one of these members suffer, all the members suffer with it; and if one is honored, all are honored with it.

THE TEMPTATION.

Luxury the perversion of beauty.—Luxury is the pleasure of possession, instead of pleasure in the thing possessed. Luxury buys things, not because it likes them, but because it likes to have them. And so the luxurious man fills his house [94]with all sorts of things, not because he finds delight in these particular things, and wants to share that delight with all his friends; but because he supposes these are the proper things to have, and he wants everybody to know that he has them.

The man who buys things in this way does not know what he wants. Consequently he gets cheated. He buys ugly things as readily as beautiful things, if only the seller is shrewd enough to make him believe they are fashionable. Others, less intelligent than this man, see what he has done; take for granted that because he has done it, it must be the proper thing to do; and go and do likewise. Thus taste becomes dulled and deadened; the costly and elaborate drives out the plain and simple; the desire for luxury kills out the love of beauty; and art expires.

THE VICE OF DEFECT.

Ugly surroundings make ugly souls.—The outward and the inward are bound fast together. The beauty or ugliness of the objects we have about us are the standing choices of our wills. As the object, so is the subject. We grow into the likeness of what we look upon. Without harmony and beauty to feed upon, the love of beauty starves and dies. Our hearts become cold and hard. Not being called out in admiration and delight, our feelings brood over mean and sensual pleasures; they dwell upon narrow and selfish concerns; they fasten upon the accumulation of wealth or the [95]vanquishing of a rival, as substitutes for the nobler interests that have vanished; and the heart becomes sordid, sensual, mean, petty, spiteful, and ugly. The spirit of man, like nature, abhors a vacuum; and into the heart from which the love of the beautiful has been suffered to depart, these hideous and ugly traits of character make haste to enter, and occupy the vacant space. What Shakspere says of a single art, music, is true of art and beauty in general:

The man that hath no music in himself,Nor is not mov'd with concord of sweet sounds,Is fit for treasons, stratagems, and spoils:The motions of his spirit are dull as night,And his affections dark as Erebus.Let no such man be trusted.

THE VICE OF EXCESS.

The hollowness of ostentation.—Man is never proud of what he really enjoys; never vain of what he truly loves; never anxious to show off the tastes and interests that are essentially his own. In order to take this false attitude toward an object, it is necessary to hold it apart from ourselves: a thing which the true lover can never do. He who loves beautiful things will indeed wish others to share his joy in them. But this sharing of our joy in beautiful objects, is a very different thing from showing off our fine things, simply to let other people know that we have them. Ostentation is the vice of ignorant wealth and vulgar luxury. It estimates objects by their expensiveness rather than by their [96]beauty; it aims to awaken in ourselves pride rather than pleasure; and to arouse in others astonishment rather than admiration.

THE PENALTY.

Vulgarity akin to laziness.—Art, and the beauty which it creates, costs painstaking labor to produce. And to enjoy it when it is produced, requires at first thoughtful and discriminating attention. The formation of a correct taste is a growth, not a gift. Hence the dull, the lazy, and the indifferent never acquire this cultivated taste for the beautiful in art. This lack of perception, this incapacity for enjoyment of the beautiful, is vulgarity. Vulgarity is contentment with what is common, and to be had on easy terms. The root of it is laziness. The mark of it is stupidity.

At great pains the race has worked out beautiful forms of speech, for communicating our ideas to each other. Vulgarity in speech is too lazy to observe these precise and beautiful forms of expression; it clips its words; throws its sentences together without regard to grammar; falls into slang; draws its figures from the coarse and low and sensual side of life, instead of from its pure and noble aspects.

Vulgarity with reference to dress, dwellings, pictures, reading, is of the same nature. It results from the dull, unmeaning gaze with which one looks at things; the shiftless, slipshod way of doing work; the "don't care" habit of mind which calls anything that happens to fall in its way "good enough."

[97] From all that is precious and beautiful and lovely the vulgar man is hopelessly excluded. They are all around him; but he has no eyes to see, no taste to appreciate, no heart to respond to them. "All things excellent," so Spinoza tells us, "are as difficult as they are rare." The vulgar man has no heart for difficulty; and hence the rare excellence of art and beauty remain forever beyond his reach.

---

[98]

CHAPTER XIII.

Animals.

Animals stand midway between things and persons. We own them, use them, kill them, even, for our own purposes. Yet they have feelings, impulses, and affections in common with ourselves. In some respects they surpass us. In strength, in speed, in keenness of scent, in fidelity, blind instinct in the animal is often superior to reason in the man.

Yet the animal falls short of personality. It is conscious, but not self-conscious. It knows; but it does not know that it knows. It can perform astonishing feats of intelligence. But it cannot explain, even to itself, the way in which it does them. The animal can pass from one particular experience to another along lines of association in time and space with marvelous directness and accuracy. To rise from a particular experience to the universal class to which that experience belongs; and then, from the known characteristics of the class, to deduce the characteristics of another particular experience of the same kind, is beyond the power of the brute.

The brute likewise has feelings; but it does not recognize these feelings as parts of a total and permanent self. Pleasure and pain the animal feels [99]probably as keenly as we do. Of happiness or unhappiness they probably know nothing.

They do not sweat and whine about their condition,They do not lie awake in the dark and weep for their sins,Not one is respectable or unhappy over the whole earth.

Animals can be trained to do right, but they cannot love righteousness. They can be trained to avoid acts which are associated with painful consequences, but they cannot hate iniquity. The life of an animal is a series of sensations, impulses, thoughts, and actions. These are never gathered up into unity. The animal is more than a machine, and less than a person.

THE DUTY.

We ought to realize that the animal has feelings as keen as our own.—We owe to these feelings in the animal the same treatment that we would wish for the same feelings in ourselves. For animals as for ourselves we should seek as much pleasure and as little pain as is consistent with the performance of the work which we think it best to lay upon them. The horse cannot choose for itself how heavy a load to draw. We ought to adapt the load to its strength. And in order to do that we must stop and consider how much strength it has. The horse and cow and dog cannot select their own food and shelter. We must think for them in these matters; and in order to do so wisely, we must consider their nature, habits, and capacities. No [100]person is fit to own an animal, who is not willing to take the trouble to understand the needs, capacities, and nature of that animal. And acts which result from ignorance of such facts as can be readily learned are inexcusable.

THE VIRTUE.

Kindness is the recognition that a feeling of another being is of just as much consequence as a feeling of my own.—Now we have seen that in some respects animals are precisely like ourselves. Kindness recognizes this bond of the kind, or kinship, as far as it extends. Kindness to animals does not go so far as kindness to our fellow-men; because the kinship between animals and man does not extend as far as kinship between man and man. So far as it does extend, however, kindness to animals treats them as we should wish to be treated by a person who had us in his power. Kindness will inflict no needless suffering upon an animal; make no unreasonable requirement of it; expose it to no needless privation.

THE REWARD.

Kindness toward animals reacts upon our hearts, making them tender and sympathetic.—Every act we perform leaves its trace in tendency to act in the same way again. And in its effect upon ourselves it matters little whether the objects on which our kindness has been bestowed have been high or low in the scale of being. In any case the effect remains with us in increased [101]tenderness, not only toward the particular objects which have called it forth, but toward all sentient beings. Kindness to animals opens our hearts toward God and our fellow-men.

He prayeth well, who loveth wellBoth man and bird and beast.

He prayeth best who loveth bestAll things both great and small;For the dear God who loveth us,He made and loveth all.

THE TEMPTATION.

We are tempted to forget this sensitive nature of the animal, and to treat it as a mere thing.—We have a perfect right to sacrifice the pleasure of an animal to the welfare of ourselves. We have no right to sacrifice the welfare of the animal to our capricious feelings. We have no right to neglect an animal from sheer unwillingness to give it the reasonable attention which is necessary to provide it with proper food, proper care, proper shelter, and proper exercise. A little girl, reproved for neglecting to feed her rabbits, when asked indignantly by her father, "Don't you love your rabbits?" replied, "Yes, I love them better than I love to feed them." This love which doesn't love to feed is sentimentality, the fundamental vice of all personal relations, of which we shall hear more later. The temptation arises even here in our relations to the animal. It is always so much easier to neglect a claim made upon us from without, than to realize and respect it.

[102] THE VICE OF DEFECT.

Ignorant or willful disregard of the nature and welfare of an animal is cruelty.—Overloading beasts of burden; driving them when lame; keeping them on insufficient food, or in dark, cold, and unhealthy quarters; whipping, goading, and beating them constantly and excessively are the most common forms of cruelty to animals. Pulling flies to pieces, stoning frogs, robbing birds' nests are forms of cruelty of which young children are often guilty before they are old enough to reflect that their sport is purchased at the cost of frightful pain to these poor innocent and defenseless creatures. The simple fact that we are strong and they are weak ought to make evident, to anyone capable of the least reflection, how mean a thing it is to take advantage of our superior strength and knowledge to inflict pain on one of these creatures which nature has placed under the protection of our superior power and knowledge, and lead us to resolve

Never to blend our pleasure or our prideWith sorrow of the meanest thing that feels.

THE VICE OF EXCESS.

Subjection to animals degrading.—The animals are vastly inferior to man in dignity and worth. Many of them have strong wills of their own, and if we will allow it, will run over us, and have their own way in spite of us. Such subjection of a man or woman to an animal is a most shameful sight. To [103]have dominion over them is man's prerogative; and to surrender that prerogative is to abrogate our humanity.

This subjection of a person to an animal may come about through a morbid and sentimental affection for an animal. When a man or a woman makes an animal so much of a pet that every caprice of the cat or dog is law; when the whole arrangements of the household are made to yield to its whims; when affections that are withheld from earnest work and human service are lavished in profusion on a pug or a canary; there again we see the order of rank in the scale of dignity and worth inverted, and the human bowing to the beast.

THE PENALTY.

Inhumanity to brutes brutalizes humanity.—If we refuse by consideration and kindness to lift the brute up into our human sympathy, and recognize in it the rights and feelings which it has in common with us, then we sink to the unfeeling and brutal level to which our cruelty seeks to consign the brutes. Every cruel blow inflicted on an animal leaves an ugly scar in our own hardened hearts, which mars and destroys our capacity for the gentlest and sweetest sympathy with our fellow-men.

---

[104]

CHAPTER XIV.

Fellow-men.

"*Unus homo, nullus homo*" is a Latin proverb which means that one man alone is no man at all. A man who should be neither son, brother, husband, father, neighbor, citizen, or friend is inconceivable. To try to think of such a man is like trying to think of a stone without size, weight, surface, or color. Man is by nature a social being. Apart from society man would not be man. "Whosoever is delighted in solitude is either a wild beast or a god." To take out of a man all that he gets from his relations to other men would be to take out of him kindness, compassion, sympathy, love, loyalty, devotion, gratitude, and heroism. It would reduce him to the level of the brutes. What water is to the fish, what air is to the bird, that association with his fellow-men is to a man. It is as necessary to the soul as food and raiment are to the body. Only as we see ourselves reflected in the praise or blame, the love or hate of others do we become conscious of ourselves.

THE DUTY.

Since our fellow-men are so essential to us and we to them, it is our duty to live in as intimate fellowship with them as possible.—The [105]fundamental form of fellowship is hospitality. By the fireside and around the family table we feel most free, and come nearest to one another. Without hospitality, such intercourse is impossible. Hospitality, in order to fulfill its mission of fellowship, must be genuine, sincere, and simple. True hospitality welcomes the guest to our hearts as well as to our homes; and the invitation to our homes when our hearts are withheld is a hollow mockery. It is a dangerous thing to have our bodies where our hearts are not. For we acquire the habit of concealing our real selves, and showing only the surface of our natures to others. We become hollow, unreal, hypocritical. We live and move

Trick'd in disguises, alien to the restOf men and alien to ourselves—and yetThe same heart beats in every human breast.

Fellowship requires not only that we shall be hospitable and ask others to our homes, but that we shall go out of our way to meet others in their homes, and wherever they may be.

The deepest fellowship cannot be made to order. It comes of itself along lines of common interests and common aims.—The harder we try to force people together, and to make them like each other, the farther they fly apart. Give them some interest or enthusiasm in common, whether it be practical, or scientific, or literary, or artistic, or musical, or religious, and this interest, which draws both toward itself at the same time [106]draws them toward each other. Hence a person, who from bashfulness or any other reason is kept from intimate fellowship with others, will often find the best way to approach them, not to force himself into their companionship, against his will and probably against theirs; but to acquire skill as a musician, or reader, or student of science or letters, or philanthropy or social problems. Then along these lines of common interest he will meet men in ways that will be at once helpful and natural.

THE VIRTUE.

Love is not soft, sentimental self-indulgence. It is going out of ourselves, and taking others into our hearts and lives.—Love calls for hard service and severe self-sacrifice, when the needs of others make service possible and self-sacrifice necessary. Love binds us to others and others to ourselves in bonds of mutual fidelity and helpfulness. A Latin poet sums up the spirit of love in the famous line:

Homo sum: humani nil a me alienum puto.[I am a man: and I count nothing human foreign to myself.]

Kant has expressed the principle of love in the form of a maxim: "Treat humanity, whether in thyself or in others, always as an end, never as a means." We have seen that the temptation to treat others merely as tools to minister to our gratification, or as obstacles to be pushed out of our pathway, is very strong. What makes us treat [107]people in that way is our failure to enter into their lives, to see things as they see them, and to feel things as they feel them. Kant tells us that we should always act with a view to the way others will be affected by it. We must treat men as men, not as things. This sympathy and appreciation for another is the first step in love. If we think of our neighbor as he thinks of himself we cannot help wishing him well. As Professor Royce says, "If he is real like thee, then is his life as bright a light, as warm a fire, to him, as thine to thee; his will is as full of struggling desires, of hard problems, of fateful decisions; his pains are as hateful, his joys as dear. Take whatever thou knowest of desire and of striving, of burning love and of fierce hatred, realize as fully as thou canst what that means, and then with clear certainty add: Such as that is for me, so it is for him, nothing less. Then thou hast known what he truly is, a Self like thy present self."

The Golden Rule, Do unto others as you would that they should do unto you, is the best summary of duty. And the keeping of that rule is possible only in so far as we love others. We must put ourselves in their place, before we can know how to treat them as we would like to be treated. And this putting self in the place of another is the very essence of love. Thou shalt love thy neighbor as thyself includes all social law. Love is the fulfilling of the law.

Love takes different forms in different [108]circumstances and in different relations. To the hungry love gives food; to the thirsty drink; to the naked clothes; to the sick nursing; to the ignorant instruction; to the blind guidance; to the erring reproof; to the penitent forgiveness. Indeed, the social virtues which will occupy the remainder of this book are simply applications of love in differing relations and toward different groups and institutions.

THE REWARD.

Love the only true bond of union between persons.—The desire to be in unity with our fellow-men is, as John Stuart Mill tells us, "already a powerful principle in human nature, and happily one of those which tend to become more strong, even without express inculcation, from the influences of advancing civilization. The deeply rooted conception which every individual even now has of himself as a social being, tends to make him feel it one of his natural wants that there should be harmony between his feelings and aims and those of his fellow-creatures." The life of love is in itself a constant realization of this deepest and strongest desire of our nature. Love is the essence of social and spiritual life; and that life of unity with our fellow-men which love creates is in itself love's own reward. "Life is energy of love." Oneness with those we love is the only goal in which love could rest satisfied. For love is "the greatest thing in the world," and any reward other than union with its object would be a loss rather than a gain.

[109] THE TEMPTATION.

Kant remarks that a dove, realizing that the resistance of the air is the sole obstacle to its progress, might imagine that if it could only get away from the air altogether, it would fly with infinite rapidity and ease.—But in fact, if the air were withdrawn for an instant it would fall helpless to the ground. Friction is the only thing the locomotive has to overcome. And if the locomotive could reason it might think how fast it could travel if only friction were removed. But without friction the locomotive could not stir a hair's breadth from the station.

In like manner, inasmuch as the greater part of our annoyances and trials and sufferings come from contact with our fellow-men, it often seems to us that if we could only get away from them altogether, and live in utter indifference to them, our lives would move on with utmost smoothness and serenity. In fact, if these relations were withdrawn, if we could attain to perfect indifference to our fellows, our life as human and spiritual beings would that instant cease.

The temptation to treat our fellow-men with indifference, like all temptations, is a delusion and leads to our destruction. Yet it is a very strong temptation to us all at times. When people do not appreciate us, and do not treat us with due kindness and consideration, it is so easy to draw into our shell and say, "I don't care a straw for them or their [110]good opinion anyway." This device is an old one. The Stoics made much of it; and boasted of the completeness of their indifference. But it is essentially weak and cowardly. It avoids certain evils, to be sure. It does so, however, not by overcoming them in brave, manly fashion; but by running and hiding away from them—an easy and a disgraceful thing to do. Intimate fellowship and close contact with others does bring pains as well as pleasures. It is the condition of completeness and fullness of moral and spiritual life; and the man who will live at his best must accept these pains with courage and resolution.

THE VICE OF DEFECT.

The outcome of indifference and lack of sympathy and fellowship is selfishness.—Unless we first feel another's interests as he feels them, we cannot help being more interested in our own affairs than we are in his, and consequently sacrificing his interests to our own when the two conflict. As George Eliot tells us in "Adam Bede," "Without this fellow-feeling, how are we to get enough patience and charity toward our stumbling, falling companions in the long, changeful journey? And there is but one way in which a strong, determined soul can learn it, by getting his heart-strings bound round the weak and erring, so that he must share not only the outward consequence of their error, but their inward suffering. That is a long and hard lesson."

It is impossible to overcome selfishness directly.—As long as our poor, private interests [111]are the only objects vividly present to our imagination and feeling, we must be selfish. The only remedy is the indirect one of entering into fellowship with others, interesting ourselves in what interests them, sharing their joys and sorrows, their hopes and fears. When we have done that, then there is something besides our petty and narrow personal interests before our minds and thoughts; and so we are in a way to get something besides mean and selfish actions from our wills and hands. We act out what is in us. If there is nothing but ourselves present to our thoughts, we shall be selfish of necessity; and without even knowing that we are selfish. If our thoughts and feelings are full of the welfare and interests of others we shall do loving and unselfish deeds, without ever stopping to think that they are loving and unselfish. Hence the precept, "Keep thy heart with all diligence, for out of it are the issues of life." A heart and mind full of sympathy and fellow-feeling is the secret of a loving life; and an idle mind and an empty heart, to which no thrill of sympathy with others is ever admitted, is the barren and desolate region from which loveless looks and cruel words and selfish deeds come forth.

Love is not a virtue which we can cultivate in ourselves by direct effort of will, and then take credit for afterward.—Love comes to us of itself; it springs up spontaneously within our breasts. We can prepare our hearts for its entrance; we can welcome and cherish it when it comes. We cannot [112]boast of it, for we could not help it. Love is the welling up within us of our true social nature; which nothing but our indifference and lack of sympathy could have kept so long repressed. "Love vaunteth not itself, is not puffed up, doth not behave itself unseemly, seeketh not its own." Love "seeketh not its own" because it has no own to seek.

Selfishness on the contrary knows all about itself; has a good opinion of itself; never gets its own interests mixed up with those of anybody else; can always give a perfectly satisfactory account of itself.

Hence when we know exactly how we came to do a thing, and appreciate keenly how good it was of us to do it; and think how very much obliged the other person ought to be to us for doing it, we may be pretty sure that it was not love, but some more or less subtle form of selfishness that prompted it. Love and selfishness may do precisely the same things. Under the influence of either love or selfishness I may "bestow all my goods to feed the poor and give my body to be burned," but love alone profiteth; while all the subtle forms of selfishness and self-seeking are "sounding brass and clanging cymbal." Selfishness, even when it does a service, has its eye on its own merit, or the reward it is to gain. In so doing it forfeits merit and reward both. Selfishness never succeeds in getting outside of itself. From all the joys and graces of the social life it remains in perpetual banishment. [113]Love loses itself in the object loved, and so finds a larger and better self. Selfishness tries to use the object of its so-called love as a means to its own gratification, and so remains to the end in loveless isolation. Many manifestations of selfishness look very much like love. To know the real difference is the most fundamental moral insight. On it depend the issues of life and death.

THE VICE OF EXCESS.

The most flagrant mockery of love is sentimentality.—The sentimentalist is on hand wherever there is a chance either to mourn or to rejoice. He is never so happy as when he is pouring forth a gush of feeling; and it matters little whether it be laughter or tears, sorrow or joy, to which he is permitted to give vent. On the surface he seems to be overflowing with the milk of human kindness. He strikes us at first sight as the very incarnation of tenderness and love.

And yet we soon discover that he cares nothing for us, or for our joys and sorrows in themselves. Anybody else, or any other occasion, would serve his purpose as well, and call forth an equal copiousness of sympathy and tears. Indeed a first rate novel, with its suffering heroine, or a good play with its pathetic scenes, would answer his purpose quite as well as any living person or actual situation. What he cares for is the thrill of emotional excitement and the ravishing sensation which accompanies all deep and tender feeling. Not love, but love's [114]delights; not sympathy, but the rapture of the sympathetic mood; not helpfulness, but the sense of self-importance which comes from being around when great trials are to be met and fateful decisions are to be made; not devotion to others, but the complacency with self which intimate connection with others gives: these are the objects at which the sentimentalist really aims.

The sentimentalist makes himself a nuisance to others and soon becomes disgusted with himself.—He cannot be relied upon for any serious service, for this gush of sentimental feeling is a transient and fluctuating thing; it gives out just as soon as it meets with difficulty and occasion for self-sacrifice. And this attempt to live forever on the topmost wave of emotional excitement defeats itself by the satiety and ennui which it brings. Whether in courtship, or society, or business, it behooves us to be on our guard against this insidious sham which cloaks selfishness in protestations of affection; pays compliments to show off its own ability to say pretty things; and undertakes responsibilities to make the impression of being of some consequence in the world. The man or woman is extremely fortunate who has never fallen a victim to this hollow mockery of love, either in self or others. The worst effect of sentimentality is that when we have detected it a few times, either in ourselves or in others, we are tempted to conclude that fellowship itself is a farce, love a delusion, and all sympathy and tenderness a weakness and a sham. [115]Every good thing has its counterfeit. By all means let this counterfeit be driven from circulation as fast as possible. But let us not lose faith in human fellowship and human love because this base imitation is so hollow and disgusting:

For life, with all it yields of joy and woe,And hope and fear,—believe the aged friend,—Is just our chance o' the prize of learning love,How love might be, hath been indeed, and is;And that we hold thenceforth to the uttermostSuch prize despite the envy of the world,And having gained truth, keep truth, that is all.

THE PENALTY.

The penalty of selfishness is strife.—The selfish man can neither leave men entirely alone, nor can he live at peace and in unity with them. Hence come strife and division. Being unwilling to make the interests of others his own, the selfish man's interests must clash with the interests of others. His hand is against every man; and every man's hand, unless it is stayed by generosity and pity, is against him. This clashing of outside interests is reflected in his own consciousness; and the war of his generous impulses with his selfish instincts makes his own breast a perpetual battlefield. The lack of harmony with his fellows in the outward world makes peace within his own soul impossible. The selfish man, by cutting himself off from his true relations with his fellow-men, cuts up the roots of the only principles which could give to his own life dignity and harmony and peace. [116]Selfishness defeats itself. By refusing to go out of self into the lives of others, the selfish man renders it impossible for the great life of human sympathy and fellowship and love to enter his own life, and fill it with its own largeness and sweetness and serenity. The selfish man remains to the last an alien, an outcast and an enemy, banished from all that is best in the life of his fellows by the insuperable obstacle of his own unwillingness to be one with them in mutual helpfulness and service.

---

[117]

CHAPTER XV.

The Poor.

Our fellow-men are so numerous and their conditions are so diverse that it is necessary to consider some of the classes and conditions of men by themselves; and to study some of the special forms which fellowship and love assume under these differing circumstances.

Of these classes or divisions in which we may group our fellow-men, the one having the first claim upon us by virtue of its greater need is the poor. The causes of poverty are accident, sickness, inability to secure work, laziness, improvidence, intemperance, ignorance, and shiftlessness. Those whose poverty is due to the first three causes are commonly called the worthy poor.

THE DUTY.

Whether worthy or unworthy, the poor are our brothers and sisters; and on the ground of our common humanity we owe them our help and sympathy.—It is easier to sympathize with the worthy than with the unworthy poor. Yet the poor who are poor as the result of their own fault are really the more in need of our pity and help. The work of lifting them up to the level of self-respect [118]and self-support is much harder than the mere giving them material relief. Yet nothing less than this is our duty. The mere tossing of pennies to the tramp and the beggar is not by any means the fulfillment of their claim upon us. Indeed, such indiscriminate giving does more harm than good. It increases rather than relieves pauperism. So that the first duty of charity is to refuse to give in this indiscriminate way. Either we must give more than food and clothes and money; or else we must give nothing at all. Indiscriminate giving merely adds fuel to the flame.

THE VIRTUE.

The special form which love takes when its object is the poor is called benevolence or charity.—True benevolence, like love, of which it is a special application, makes the well-being of its object its own. In what then does the well-being of the poor consist? Is it bread and beef, a coat on the back, a roof over the head, and a bed to sleep in? These are conditions of well-being, but not the whole of it. A man cannot be well off without these things. But it is by no means sure that he will be well off with them.

What a man thinks; how he feels; what he loves; what he hopes for; what he is trying to do; what he means to be;—these are quite as essential elements in his well-being as what he has to eat and wear. True benevolence therefore must include these things in its efforts. Benevolence must aim to improve the [119]man together with his condition or its gifts will be worse than wasted.

There are three principles which all wise benevolence must observe.

First: Know all that can be known about the man you help.—Unless we are willing to find out all we can about a poor man, we have no business to indulge our sympathy or ease our conscience by giving him money or food. It is often easier to give than to withhold. But it is far more harmful. When Bishop Potter says that "It is far better,—better for him and better for us,—to give a beggar a kick than to give him a half-dollar," it sounds like a hard saying, yet it is the strict truth. In a civilized and Christian community any really deserving person can secure assistance through persons or agencies that either know about his needs, or will take the trouble to look them up. When a stranger begs from strangers he thereby confesses that he prefers to present his claims where their merits are unknown; and the act proclaims him as a fraud. To the beggar, to ourselves, and to the really deserving poor, we owe a prompt and stern refusal of all uninvestigated appeals for charity. "True charity never opens the heart without at the same time opening the mind."

The second principle is: Let the man you help know as much as he can of you.—Bureaus and societies are indispensable aids to effective benevolence; without their aid thorough knowledge of the needs and merits of the poor would be impossible. [120]Their function, however, should be to direct and superintend, not to dispense with and supplant direct personal contact between giver and receiver. The recipient of aid should know the one who helps him as man or woman, not as secretary or agent. If all the money, food, and clothing necessary to relieve the wants of the poor could be deposited at their firesides regularly each Christmas by Santa Claus, such a Christmas present, with the regular expectation of its repetition each year, would do these poor families more harm than good. It might make them temporarily more comfortable; it would make them permanently less industrious, thrifty, and self-reliant.

Investigations have proved conclusively that half the persons who are in want in our cities need no help at all, except help in finding work. One-sixth are unworthy of any material assistance whatever, since they would spend it immediately on their vices. One-fifth need only temporary help and encouragement to get over hard places. Only about one-tenth need permanent assistance.

On the other hand all need cheer, comfort, advice, sympathy, and encouragement, or else reproof, warning, and restraint. They all need kind, firm, wise, judicious friends. The less professionalism, the more personal sympathy and friendliness there is in our benevolence, the better it will be. In the words of Octavia Hill: "It is the families, the homes of the poor that need to be influenced. Is not she most sympathetic, most powerful, who nursed her own mother through her long illness, and knew how to [121]go quietly through the darkened room: who entered so heartily into her sister's marriage: who obeyed so heartily her father's command when it was hardest? Better still if she be wife and mother herself and can enter into the responsibilities of a head of a household, understands her joys and cares, knows what heroic patience it needs to keep gentle when the nerves are unhinged and the children noisy. Depend upon it if we thought of the poor primarily as husbands, wives, sons, daughters, members of households as we are ourselves, instead of contemplating them as a different class, we should recognize better how the home training and the high ideal of home duty was our best preparation for work among them."

The third principle is: Give the man you help no more and no less than he needs to make his life what you and he together see that it is good for it to be.—This principle shows how much to give. Will ten cents serve as an excuse for idleness? Will five cents be spent in drink? Will one cent relax his determination to earn an honest living for himself and family? Then these sums are too much, and should be withheld. On the other hand, can the man be made hopeful, resolute, determined to overcome the difficulties of a trying situation? Can you impart to him your own strong will, your steadfast courage, your high ideal? is he ready to work, and willing to make any sacrifice that is necessary to regain the power of self-support? Then you will not count any sum that you can afford to [122]give too great; even if it be necessary to carry him and his family right through a winter by sheer force of giving outright everything they need.

It is not the amount of the gift, but the spirit in which it is received that makes it good or bad for the recipient. If received by a man who clings to all the weakness and wickedness that brought his poverty upon him, then your gift, whether small or large, does no good and much harm. If with the gift the man welcomes your counsel, follows your advice, adopts your ideal, and becomes partaker in your determination that he shall become as industrious, and prudent, and courageous as a man in his situation can be, then whether you give him little or much material assistance, every cent of it goes to the highest work in which wealth can be employed—the making a man more manlike.

THE REWARD.

Our attitude toward the poor and unfortunate is the test of our attitude toward humanity.—For the poor and unfortunate present humanity to us in the condition which most strongly appeals to our fellow-feeling. The way in which I treat this poor man who happens to cross my path, is the way I should treat my dearest friend, if he were equally poor and unfortunate, and equally remote from personal association with my past life. The man who will let a single poor family suffer, when he is able to afford relief, is capable of being false to the whole human race. Speaking in the name of our common [123]humanity, the Son of Man declares, "Inasmuch as ye have done it unto one of the least of these my brethren, ye have done it unto me." Sympathy "doubles our joys and halves our sorrows." It increases our range of interest and affection, making "the world one fair moral whole" in which we share the joys and sorrows of our brothers.

The man who sympathizes with the sufferings of others seeks and finds the sympathy of others in his own losses and trials when they come.—Familiarity and sympathy with the sufferings of others strengthens us to bear suffering when it comes to us: for we are able to see that it is no unusual and exceptional evil falling upon us alone, but accept it as an old and familiar acquaintance, whom we have so often met in other lives that we do not fear his presence in our own.

THE TEMPTATION.

"Am I my brother's keeper?"—We are comfortable and well cared for. We are earning our own living. We pay our debts. We work hard for what we get. Why should we not enjoy ourselves? Why should I share my earnings with the shiftless vagabond, the good-for-nothing loafer? What is he to me? In one or another of these forms the murderous question "Am I my brother's keeper?" is sure to rise to our lips when the needs of the poor call for our assistance and relief. Or if we do recognize the claim, we are tempted to hide behind some organization; giving our money to that; and sending [124]it to do the actual work. We do not like to come into the real presence of suffering and want. We do not want to visit the poor man in his tenement; and clasp his hand, and listen with our own ears to the tale of wretchedness and woe as it falls directly from his lips. We do not care to take the heavy and oppressive burden of his life's problem upon our own minds and hearts. We wish him well. But we do not will his betterment strongly and earnestly enough to take us to his side, and join our hands with his in lifting off the weight that keeps him down. Alienation, the desire to hold ourselves aloof from the real wretchedness of our brother, is our great temptation with reference to the poor.

THE VICE OF DEFECT.

The reluctant doling out of insufficient aid to the poor is niggardliness.—The niggard is thinking all the time of himself, and how he hates to part with what belongs to him. He gives as little as he can; and that little hurts him terribly. This vice cannot be overcome directly. It is a phase of selfishness; and like all forms of selfishness it can be cured only by getting out of self into another's life. By going among the poor, studying their needs, realizing their sufferings, we may be drawn out of our niggardliness and find a pleasure in giving which we could never have cultivated by direct efforts of will. We cannot make ourselves benevolent by making up our minds that we will be [125]benevolent. Like all forms of love, benevolence cannot be forced; but it will come of itself if we give its appropriate objects a large share of our thoughts and a warm place in our hearts.

THE VICE OF EXCESS.

Regard for others as they happen to be, instead of regard for what they are capable of becoming, leads to soft hearted and mischievous indulgence.—The indulgent giver sees the fact of suffering and rushes to its relief, without stopping to inquire into the cause of the poverty and the best measures of relief. Indulgence fails to see the ideal of what the poor man is to become. Indulgence does not look beyond the immediate fact of poverty; and consequently the indulgent giver does nothing to lift the poor man out of it. Help in poverty, rather than help out of poverty, is what indulgent giving amounts to. The indulgent and indiscriminate giver becomes a partner in the production of poverty. This indulgent giving is a phase of sentimentality; and the relief of one's own feelings, rather than the real good of a fellow-man is at the root of all such mischievous almsgiving. It is the form of benevolence without the substance. It does too much for the poor man just because it loves him too little. Indulgence measures benefactions, not by the needs and capacities of the receiver, but by the sensibilities and emotions of the giver. What wonder that it always goes astray, and does harm under the guise of doing good!

[126] THE PENALTY.

Uncharitable treatment of the poor makes us alien to humanity, and distrustful of human nature.—We feel that they have a claim upon us that we have not fulfilled; and we try to push them off beyond the range of our sympathy. They are not slow to take the hint. They interpret our harsh tones and our cold looks, and they look to us for help no more. But in pushing these poor ones beyond our reach, we unconsciously acquire hard, unsympathetic ways of thinking, feeling, speaking and acting, which others not so poor, others whom we would gladly have near us, also interpret; and they too come to understand that there is no real kindness and helpfulness to be had from us in time of real need, and they keep their inmost selves apart, and suffer us to touch them only on the surface of their lives. When trouble comes to us we instinctively feel that we have no claim on the sympathy of others; and so we have to bear our griefs alone. Having never suffered with others, sorrow is a stranger to us, and we think we are the most miserable creatures in the world.

Humanity is one. Action and reaction are equal. Our treatment of the poorest of our fellows is potentially our treatment of them all. And by a subtle law of compensation, which runs deeper than our own consciousness, what our attitude is toward our fellows determines their attitude toward us. "Inasmuch as ye did it not to one of the least of these my brethren," says the Representative of our common humanity, "ye did it not unto me."

---

[127]

CHAPTER XVI.

Wrongdoers.

Another class of our fellow-men whom it is especially hard to love are those who willfully do wrong. The men who cheat us, and say hateful things to us; the men who abuse their wives and neglect their families; the men who grind the faces of the poor, and contrive to live in ease and luxury on the earnings of the widow and the orphan; the men who pervert justice and corrupt legislation in order to make money; these and all wrongdoers exasperate us, and rouse our righteous indignation. Yet they are our fellow-men. We meet them everywhere. We suffer for their misdeeds;—and, what is worse, we have to see others, weaker and more helpless than ourselves, maltreated, plundered, and beaten by these wretches and villains. Wrongdoing is a great, hard, terrible fact. We must face it. We must have some clear and consistent principles of action with reference to these wrongdoers; or else our wrath and indignation will betray us into the futile attempt to right one wrong by another wrong; and so drag us down to the level of the wrongdoers against whom we contend.

[128] THE DUTY.

The first thing we owe to the wrongdoer is to give him his just deserts. Wrongdoing always hurts somebody. Justice demands that it shall hurt the wrongdoer himself.—The boy who tells a lie treats us as if we did not belong to the same society, and have the same claim on truth that he has. We must make him feel that we do not consider him fit to be on a level with us. We must make him ashamed of himself. The man who cheats us shows that he is willing to sacrifice our interests to his. We must show him that we will have no dealings with such a person. The man who is mean and stingy shows that he cares nothing for us. We must show him that we despise his miserliness and meanness. The robber and the murderer show that they are enemies to society. Society must exclude them from its privileges.

It is the function of punishment to bring the offender to a realizing sense of the nature of his deed, by making him suffer the natural consequences of it, or an equivalent amount of privation, in his own person. Punishment is a favor to the wrongdoer, just as bitter medicine is a favor to the sick. For without it, he would not appreciate the evil of his wrongdoing with sufficient force to repent of it, and abandon it. Plato teaches the true value of punishment in the "Gorgias." "The doing of wrong is the greatest of evils. To suffer punishment is the way to be released from this evil.

[129]Not to suffer is to perpetuate the evil. To do wrong, then, is second only in the scale of evils; but to do wrong and not to be punished, is first and greatest of all. He who has done wrong and has not been punished, is and ought to be the most miserable of all men; the doer of wrong is more miserable than the sufferer; and he who escapes punishment more miserable than he who suffers punishment."

Punishment is the best thing we can do for one who has done wrong.—Punishment is not a good in itself. But it is good relatively to the wrongdoer. It is the only way out of wrong into right. Punishment need not be brutal or degrading. The most effectual punishment is often purely mental; consisting in the sense of shame and sorrow which the offender is made to feel. In some form or other every wrongdoer should be made to feel painfully the wrongness of his deed. To "spare the rod," both literally and metaphorically, is to "spoil the child." The duty of inflicting punishment, like all duty, is often hard and unwelcome. But we become partakers in every wrong which we suffer to go unpunished and unrebuked when punishment and rebuke are within our power.

THE VIRTUE.

Forgiveness is not inconsistent with justice. It does not do away with punishment. It spiritualizes punishment; substituting mental for bodily pains.—The sense of the evil and shame of [130]wrongdoing, which is the essence and end of punishment, forgiveness, when it is appreciated, serves to intensify. Indeed it is impossible to inflict punishment rightly until you have first forgiven the offender. For punishment should be inflicted for the offender's good. And not until vengeance has given way to forgiveness are we able to care for the offender's well-being.

Forgiveness is a special form of love. It recognizes the humanity of the offender, and treats him as a brother, even when his deeds are most unbrotherly. But it cares so much for him that it will not shrink from inflicting whatever merciful pains may be necessary to deliver him from his own unbrotherliness. Forgiveness loves not the offense but the man. It hates the offense chiefly because it injures the man. Its punishment of the offense is the negative side of its positive devotion to the person. The command "love your enemies" is not a hard impossibility on the one hand, nor a soft piece of sentimentalism on the other. It is possible, because there is a human, loveable side, even to the worst villain, if we can only bring ourselves to think on that better side, and the possibilities which it involves. It is practical, because regard for that better side of his nature demands that we shall make him as miserable in his wrongdoing as is necessary to lead him to abandon his wrongdoing, and give the better possibilities of his nature a chance to develop. The parent who punishes the naughty child loves him not less but more than the parent [131]who withholds the needed punishment. The state which suffers crime to go unpunished becomes a nursery of criminals. It wrongs itself; it wrongs honest citizens; but most of all it wrongs the criminals themselves whom it encourages in crime by undue lenity. The object of forgiveness is not to take away punishment, but to make whatever punishment remains effective for the reformation of the offender. It is to transfer the seat of suffering from the body, where its effect is uncertain and indirect, to the mind, where sorrow for wrongdoing is powerful and efficacious. Every wrong act brings its penalty with it. In order to induce repentance and reformation that penalty must in some way be brought home to the one who did the wrong. Vengeance drives the penalty straight home, refusing to bear any part of it itself. Forgiveness first takes the penalty upon itself in sorrow for the wrong, and then invites the wrongdoer to share the sorrow which he who forgives him has already borne. Vengeance smites the body, and often drives in deeper the perversity. Forgiveness touches the heart and gently but firmly draws the heart's affections away from the wrong, into devotion to the right.

THE REWARD.

Forgiveness, rightly received, works the reformation of the offender.—And to one who ardently loves righteousness there is no joy comparable to that of seeing a man who has been doing wrong, turn from it, renounce it, and determine that henceforth he will [132]endeavor to do right. Contrast heightens our emotions. And there is "joy over one sinner that repenteth, more than over ninety and nine righteous persons that need no repentance." Deliverance from wrong is effected by the firm yet kindly presentation of the right as something still possible for us, and into which a friend stands ready to welcome us. Reformation is wrought by that blending of justice and forgiveness which at the same time holds the wrong abhorrent and the wrongdoer dear. Reformation is the end at which forgiveness aims, and its accomplishment is its own reward.

THE TEMPTATION.

The sight of heinous offenses and outrageous deeds against ourselves or others tempts us to wreak our vengeance upon the offender.—This impulse of revenge served a useful purpose in the primitive condition of human society. It still serves as the active support of righteous indignation. But it is blind and rough; and is not suited to the conditions of civilized life. Vengeance has no consideration for the true well-being of the offender. It confounds the person with the deed in wholesale condemnation. It renders evil for evil; it provokes still further retaliation; and erects a single fault into the occasion of a lasting feud. It is irrational, brutal, and inhuman; it is dangerous and degrading.

[133] THE VICE OF DEFECT.

The absence of forgiveness in dealing with wrongdoers leads to undue severity.—The end of punishment being to bring the offender to realize the evil of his deed and to repent of it, punishment should not be carried beyond the point which is necessary to produce that result. To continue punishment after genuine penitence is manifested is to commit a fresh wrong ourselves. "If thy brother sin, rebuke him; and if he repent, forgive him. And if he sin against thee seven times in a day, and seven times turn again to thee, saying, I repent, thou shalt forgive him." To ignore an unrepented wrong, and to continue to punish a repented wrong, are equally wide of the mark of that love for the offender which metes out to him both justice and forgiveness according to his needs. All punishment which is not tempered with forgiveness is brutal; and brutalizes both punisher and punished. It hardens the heart of the offender; and itself constitutes a new offense against him.

These principles apply strictly to relations between individuals. In the case of punishment by the state, the necessity of self-protection; of warning others; and of approximate uniformity in procedure; added to the impossibility of getting at the exact state of mind of the offender by legal processes, render it necessary to inflict penalties in many cases which are more severe than the best interest of the individual offenders requires. To meet such cases, and to [134]mitigate the undue severity of uniform penalties when they fall too heavily on individuals, all civilized nations give the power of pardon to the executive.

Whether the penalty be in itself light or severe, it should always be administered in the endeavor to improve and reform the character of the offender.—The period of confinement in jail or prison should be made a period of real privation and suffering; but it should be especially the privation of opportunity for indulgence in idleness and vice; and the painfulness of discipline in acquiring the knowledge and skill necessary to make the convict a self-respecting and self-supporting member of society, after his term of sentence expires.

THE VICE OF EXCESS.

Lenity ignores the wrong; and by ignoring it, becomes responsible for its repetition.—Lenity is sentimentality bestowed on criminals. It treats them in the manner most congenial to its own feelings, instead of in the way most conducive to their good. Forgiveness is regard for the offender in view of his ability to renounce the offense and try to do better in the future.

Lenity confounds offender and offense in a wholesale and promiscuous amnesty. The true attitude toward the wrongdoer must preserve the balance set forth by the lawgiver of Israel as characteristic of Israel's God, "full of compassion and gracious, slow to anger and plenteous [135]in mercy and truth; keeping mercy for thousands, forgiving iniquity and transgression and sin: and *that will by no means clear the guilty*." Lenity which "clears the guilty" is neither mercy, nor graciousness, nor compassion, nor forgiveness. Such lenity obliterates moral distinctions; disintegrates society; corrupts and weakens the moral nature of the one who indulges in it; and confirms in perversity him on whom it is bestowed.

THE PENALTY.

Severity and lenity alike increase the perversity of the offender.— Severity drives the offender into fresh determination to do wrong; and intrenches him behind the conception that he has been treated unfairly. He is made to think that all the world is against him, and he sees no reason why he should not set himself against the world. Lenity leads him to think the world is on his side no matter what he does; and so he asks himself why he should take the trouble to mend his ways. Lenity to others leads us to be lenient toward ourselves; and we commit wrong in expectation of that lenient treatment which we are in the habit of according to others. Severity to others makes us ashamed to ask for mercy when we need it for ourselves. Furthermore, knowing there is no mercy in ourselves, we naturally infer that there is none in others. We disbelieve in forgiveness; and our disbelief hides from our eyes the forgiveness, which, if we had [136]more faith in its presence, we might find. Hence the unforgiving man can find no forgiveness for himself in time of need; he sinks to that level of despair and confirmed perversity, to which his own unrelenting spirit has doomed so many of his erring brothers.

---

[137]

CHAPTER XVII.

Friends.

In addition to that bond of a common humanity which ought to bind us to all our fellow-men, there is a tie of special affinity between persons of congenial tastes, kindred pursuits, common interests, and mutually cherished ideals. Persons to whom we are drawn, and who are likewise drawn to us, by these cords of subtle sympathy we call our friends.

Friendship is regard for what our friend is; not for what he can do for us. "The perfect friendship," says Aristotle, "is that of good men who resemble one another in virtue. For they both alike wish well to one another as good men, and it is their essential character to be good men. And those who wish well to their friends for the friends' sake are friends in the truest sense; for they have these sentiments toward each other as being what they are, and not in an accidental way; their friendship, therefore, lasts as long as their virtue, and that is a lasting thing. Such friendships are uncommon, for such people are rare. Such friendship requires long and familiar intercourse. For they cannot be friends till each show and approve himself to the other as worthy to be loved. A wish to be friends may be of rapid growth, but not friendship. Those [138]whose love for one another is based on the useful, do not love each other for what they are, but only in so far as each gets some good from the other. These friendships are accidental; for the object of affection is loved, not as being the person or character that he is, but as the source of some good or some pleasure. Friendships of this kind are easily dissolved, as the persons do not continue unchanged; for if they cease to be useful or pleasant to one another, their love ceases. On the disappearance of that which was the motive of their friendship, their friendship itself is dissolved, since it existed solely with a view to that. For pleasure then or profit it is possible even for bad men to be friends with one another; but it is evident that the friendship in which each loves the other for himself is only possible between good men; for bad men take no delight in each other unless some advantage is to be gained. The friendship whose motive is utility is the friendship of sordid souls. Friendship lies more in loving than in being loved; so that when people love each other in proportion to their worth, they are lasting friends, and theirs is lasting friendship."

THE DUTY.

The interest of our friend should be our interest; his welfare, our welfare; his wish, our will; his good, our aim.—If he prospers we rejoice; if he is overtaken by adversity, we must stand by him. If he is in want, we must share our goods with him. If he is unpopular, we must stand up for him. If he [139]does wrong, we must be the first to tell him of his fault: and the first to bear with him the penalty of his offense. If he is unjustly accused we must believe in his innocence to the last. Friends must have all things in common; not in the sense of legal ownership, which would be impracticable, and, as Epicurus pointed out, would imply mutual distrust; but in the sense of a willingness on the part of each to do for the other all that is in his power. Only on the high plane of such absolute, whole-souled devotion can pure friendship be maintained.

THE VIRTUE.

The true friend is one we can rely upon.—Our deepest secrets, our tenderest feelings, our frankest confessions, our inmost aspirations, our most cherished plans, our most sacred ideals are as safe in his keeping as in our own. Yes, they are safer; for the faithful friend will not hesitate to prick the bubbles of our conceit; laugh us out of our sentimentality; expose the root of selfishness beneath our virtuous pretensions. "Faithful are the wounds of a friend." To be sure the friend must do all this with due delicacy and tact. If he takes advantage of his position to exercise his censoriousness upon us we speedily vote him a bore, and take measures to get rid of him. But when done with gentleness and good nature, and with an eye single to our real good, this pruning of the tendrils of our inner life is one of the most precious offices of friendship.

[140] THE REWARD.

The chief blessing of friendship is the sense that we are not living our lives and fighting our battles alone; but that our lives are linked with the lives of others, and that the joys and sorrows of our united lives are felt by hearts that beat as one.—The seer who laid down so severely the stern conditions which the highest friendship must fulfill, has also sung its praises so sweetly, that his poem at the beginning of his essay may serve as our description of the blessings which it is in the power of friendship to confer:

A ruddy drop of manly bloodThe surging sea outweighs;The world uncertain comes and goes,The lover rooted stays.I fancied he was fled,And, after many a year,Glowed unexhausted kindlinessLike daily sunrise there.My careful heart was free again,—Oh, friend, my bosom said,Through thee alone the sky is arched,Through thee the rose is red,All things through thee take nobler formAnd look beyond the earth,The mill-round of our fate appearsA sun-path in thy worth.Me too thy nobleness has taughtTo master my despair;The fountains of my hidden lifeAre through thy friendship fair.

[141] THE TEMPTATION.

A relation so intimate as that of friendship offers constant opportunity for betrayal.—Friends understand each other perfectly. Friend utters to friend many things which he would not for all the world let others know. And more than that, the intimate association of friendship cannot fail to give the friend an opportunity to perceive the deep secrets of the other's heart which he would not speak even to a friend, and which he has scarcely dared to acknowledge even to himself.

This intimate knowledge of another appeals strangely to our vanity and pride; and we are often tempted to show it off by disclosing some of these secrets which have been revealed to us in the confidence of friendship. This is the meanest thing one person can do to another. The person who yields to this basest of temptations is utterly unworthy ever again to have a friend. Betrayal of friends is the unpardonable social sin.

THE VICE OF DEFECT.

We cannot find people who in every respect are exactly to our liking.—And, what is more to the point, we never can make ourselves exactly what we should like to have other people intimately know and understand. Friendship calls for courage enough to show ourselves in spite of our frailties and imperfections; and to take others in spite of the possible shortcomings which close acquaintance may reveal in them. Friendship requires a readiness [142]to give and take, for better or for worse; and that exclusiveness which shrinks from the risks involved is simply a combination of selfishness and cowardice. Refusal to make friends is a sure sign that a man either is ashamed of himself, or else lacks faith in his fellow-men. And these two states of mind are not so different as they might at first appear. For we judge others chiefly by ourselves. And the man who distrusts his fellow-men, generally bases his distrust of them on the consciousness that he himself is not worthy of the trust of others. So that the real root of exclusiveness is the dread of letting other people get near to us, for fear of what they might discover. Exclusiveness puts on the airs of pride. But pride is only a game of bluff, by which a man who is ashamed to have other people get near enough to see him as he is pretends that he is terribly afraid of getting near enough to others to see what they are.

THE VICE OF EXCESS.

Effusiveness.—Some people can keep nothing to themselves. As soon as they get an experience, or feel an emotion, or have an ache or pain, they must straightway run and pour it into the ear of some sympathetic listener. The result is that experiences do not gain sufficient hold upon the nature to make any deep and lasting impression. No independence, no self-reliance, no strength of character is developed. Such people are superficial and unreal. They ask everything and have nothing to give. The stream is so large and constant that there is [143]nothing left in the reservoir. Friendship must rest on solid foundations of independence and mutual respect. With great clearness and force Emerson proclaims this law in his Essay on Friendship: "We must be our own before we can be another's. Let me be alone to the end of the world, rather than that my friend should overstep, by a word or a look, his real sympathy. Let him not cease an instant to be himself. The only joy I have in his being mine, is that the not mine is mine. I hate where I looked for a manly furtherance, or at least a manly resistance, to find a mush of concession. Better be a nettle in the side of your friend than his echo. The condition which high friendship demands is ability to do without it. There must be very two, before there can be very one. Let it be an alliance of two large formidable natures, mutually beheld, mutually feared, before yet they recognize the deep identity, which, beneath these disparities, unites them."

THE PENALTY.

If we refuse to go in company there is nothing left for us but to trudge along the dreary way alone.—If we will not bear one another's burdens, we must bear our own when they are heaviest in our unaided strength; and fall beneath their weight. Here as everywhere penalty is simply the inevitable consequence of conduct. The loveless heart is doomed to drag out its term of years in the cheerless isolation of a life from which the light of love has been withdrawn.

[144]

CHAPTER XVIII.

The Family.

Thus far we have considered our fellow-men as units, with whom it is our privilege and duty to come into external relations. These external relations after all do not reach the deepest center of our lives. They indeed bind man to man in bonds of helpfulness and service. But the two who are thus united remain two separate selves after all. Even friendship leaves unsatisfied yearnings, undeveloped possibilities in human hearts. However subtle and tender the bond may be, it remains to the last physical rather than chemical; mechanical rather than vital; the outward attachment of mutually exclusive wholes, rather than the inner blending of complemental elements which lose their separate selfhood in the unity of a new and higher life. The beginning of this true spiritual life, in which the individual loses his separate self to find a larger and nobler self in a common good in which each individual shares, and which none may monopolize;—the birthplace of the soul as of the body is in the family. The nursery of virtue, the inspirer of devotion, the teacher of self-sacrifice, the institutor of love, the family is the foundation of all those higher [145]and nobler qualities of mind and heart which lift man above the level of sagacious brutes.

THE DUTY.

The family a common good.—Membership in the family involves the recognition that the true life of the individual is to be found only in union with other members; in regard for their rights; in deference to their wishes; and in devotion to that common interest in which each member shares. Each member must live for the sake of the whole family. Children owe to their parents obedience, and such service as they are able to render. Parents, on the other hand, owe to children support, training, and an education sufficient to give them a fair start in life. Brothers and sisters owe to each other mutual helpfulness and protection. All joys and sorrows, all hopes and fears, all plans and purposes should be talked over, and carried out in common. No parent should have a plan or ambition or enthusiasm into which he does not invite the confidence and sympathy of his child. No child should cherish a thought or purpose or imagination which he cannot share with father or mother. It is the duty of the parent to enter sympathetically into the sports and recreations and studies and curiosities of the child. It is the duty of the child to interest himself in whatever the father and mother are doing to support the family and promote its welfare.

Between parent and child, brother and sister, there should be no secrets; no ground on [146]which one member lives in selfish isolation from the rest.

The basis of right marriage.—These relations come by nature, and we grow into them so gradually that we are scarcely conscious of their existence, unless we stop on purpose to think of them. Marriage, or the foundation of a new family, however, is a step which we take for ourselves, once for all, in the maturity of our conscious powers. To know in advance the true from the false, the real from the artificial, the genuine from the counterfeit, the blessed from the wretched basis of marriage is the most important piece of information a young man or woman can acquire. The test is simple but searching. Do you find in another, one to whose well-being you can devote your life; one to whom you can confide the deepest interests of your mind and heart; one whose principles and purposes you can appreciate and respect: one in whose image you wish your children to be born, and on the model of whose character you wish their characters to be formed; one whose love will be the best part of whatever prosperity, and the sufficient shield against whatever adversity may be your common lot? Then, provided this other soul sees a like worth in you, and cherishes a like devotion for what you are and aim to be, marriage is not merely a duty: it is the open door into the purest and noblest life possible to man and woman. Complete identification and devotion, entire surrender of each to each in mutual affection is the condition of true marriage. As [147]"John Halifax" says in refusing the hand of a nobleman for his daughter, "In marriage there must be unity—one aim, one faith, one love—or the marriage is imperfect, unholy, a mere civil contract, and no more." This necessity of complete, undivided devotion of each to each is, as Hegel points out, the spiritual necessity on which monogamy rests. There can be but one complete and perfect and supreme merging of one's whole self in the life and love of another. Marriage with two would be of necessity marriage with none. If we apprehend the spiritual essence of marriage we see that marriage with more than one is a contradiction in terms. It is possible to cut one's self up into fragments, and bestow a part here and a part there; but that is not marriage; it is mere alliance. It brings not love and joy and peace, but hate and wretchedness and strife.

A true marriage never can be dissolved.—If love be present at the beginning it will grow stronger and richer with every added year of wedded life. How far a loveless marriage should be enforced upon unwilling parties by the state for the benefit of society is a question which it is foreign to our present purpose to discuss. The duty of the individual who finds himself or herself in this dreadful condition is, however, clear. There is generally a good deal of self-seeking on both sides at the basis of such marriages. Getting rather than giving was the real though often unsuspected hope that brought them together. If either husband or wife will [148]resolutely strive to correct the fault that is in him or her, ceasing to demand and beginning to give unselfish affection and genuine devotion, in almost every case, where the man is not a brute or a sot, and the woman is not a fashion-plate or a fiend, the life of mutual love may be awakened, and a true marriage may supersede the empty form. Not until faithful and prolonged efforts to establish a true marriage within the legal bonds have proved unavailing; and only where adultery, desertion, habitual drunkenness, or gross brutality and cruelty demonstrate the utter impossibility of a true marriage, is husband or wife justified in seeking to escape the bond, and to revert to the lower, individualistic type of life.

THE VIRTUE.

In the family we are members one of another.—The parent shows his loyalty to the child by protecting him when he gets into trouble. The loyal brother defends his brothers and sisters against all attacks and insults. The loyal child refuses to do anything contrary to the known wishes of father and mother, or anything that will reflect discredit upon them. The loyal child cares for his parents and kindred in misfortune and old age; ministering tenderly to their wants, and bearing patiently their infirmities of body and of mind which are incidental to declining powers. The loyal husband and wife trust each other implicitly in everything; and refuse to have any confidences with others more intimate [149]than they have with each other. Not that the family is narrow and exclusive. Husband and wife should each have their outside interests, friendships, and enthusiasms. Each should rejoice in everything which broadens, deepens, and sweetens the life of the other. Jealousy of each other is the most deadly poison that can be introduced into a home. It is sure and instant death to the peace and joy of married life.

Other relations should always be secondary and external to the primary and inner relation of husband and wife to each other.—It should be the married self; the self which includes in its inmost love and confidence husband or wife; not a detached and independent self, which goes out to form connections and attachments in the outer world. Where this mutual trust and confidence are loyally maintained there can be the greatest social freedom toward other men and women and at the same time perfect trust and devotion to each other. This, however, is a nice adjustment, which nothing short of perfect love can make. Love makes it easily, and as a matter of course. Loyalty is love exposed to strain, and overcoming strain and temptation by the power which love alone can give.

THE REWARD.

Loyalty to the family preserves and perpetuates the home.—Home is a place where we can rest; where we can breathe freely; where we can have perfect trust in one another; where we can be [150]perfectly simple, perfectly natural, perfectly frank; where we can be ourselves; where peace and love are supreme. "This," says John Ruskin, "is the true nature of home—it is the place of peace; the shelter, not only from all injury, but from all terror, doubt, and division. In so far as it is not this, it is not home; so far as the anxieties of the outer life penetrate into it, and the unknown, unloved, or hostile society of the outer world is allowed to cross the threshold, it ceases to be home; it is then only a part of the outer world which you have roofed over and lighted fire in. But so far as it is a sacred place, a vestal temple, a temple of the hearth watched over by household gods, before whose faces none may come but those whom they can receive with love,—so far as it is this, and roof and fire are types only of a nobler shade and light,—shade as of a rock in a weary land, and light as of a Pharos on a stormy sea; so far it vindicates the name and fulfills the praise of home."

THE TEMPTATION.

The individual must drop his extreme individualism when he crosses the threshold of the home.—The years between youth and marriage are years of comparative independence. The young man and woman learn in these years to take their affairs into their own hands; to direct their own course, to do what seems right in their own eyes, and take the consequences of wisdom or folly upon their own shoulders. This period [151]of independence is a valuable discipline. It develops strength and self-reliance; it compels the youth to face the stern realities of life, and to measure himself against the world. It helps him to appreciate what his parents have done for him in the past, and prepares him to appreciate a home of his own when he comes to have one. The man and woman who have never known what it is to make their own way in the world can never be fully confident of their own powers, and are seldom able to appreciate fully what is done for them.

Many an exacting husband and complaining wife would have had their querulousness and ingratitude taken out of them once for all if they could have had a year or two of single-handed conflict with real hardship. Independence and self-reliance are the basis of self-respect and self-control.

At the same time this habit of independence, especially if it is ingrained by years of single life, tends to perpetuate itself in ways that are injurious to the highest domestic and family life. Independence is a magnificent foundation for marriage; to carry it up above the foundation, and build the main structure out of it, is fatal. The insistence on rights, the urging of claims, the enforcement of private whims and fancies, are the death of love and the destruction of the family. Unless one is ready to give everything, asking nothing save what love gives freely in return, marriage will prove a fountain of bitterness rather than of sweetness; a region of storm and tempest rather than a haven of repose. [152]Within a bond so close and all-embracing there is no room for the independent life of separated selves. Each must lose self in the other; both must merge themselves in devotion to a common good; or the bond becomes a fetter, and the home a prison. Unless one is prepared to give all to the object of his love, duty to self, to the object of his affections, and to the blessed state of marriage demands that he should offer nothing, and remain outside a relation which his whole self cannot enter. Independence outside of marriage is respectable and honorable. Independence and self-assertion in marriage toward husband or wife is mean and cruel. It is the attempt to partake of that in which we refuse to participate; to claim the advantages of an organism in which we refuse to comply with the conditions of membership. Not admiration, nor fascination, nor sentimentality, nor flattered vanity can bind two hearts together in life-long married happiness. For these are all forms of self-seeking in disguise. Love alone, love that loses self in its object; love that accepts service with gladness and transmutes sacrifice into a joy; simple, honest, self-forgetful love must be the light and life of marriage, or else it will speedily go out in darkness and expire in death.

Of the deliberate seeking of external ends in marriage, such as money, position, family connections, and the like, it ought not to be necessary to say a word to any thoughtful person. It is the basest act of which man or woman is capable. It is an insult to marriage; it is a mockery of love; it is treachery [153]and falsehood and robbery toward the person married. It subordinates the lifelong welfare of a person to the acquisition of material things. It introduces fraud and injustice into the inmost center of one's life, and makes respect of self, happiness in marriage, faith in human nature forever impossible. The deliberate formation of a loveless marriage is a blasphemy against God, a crime against society, a wrong to a fellow being, and a bitter and lasting curse to one's own soul.

THE VICE OF DEFECT.

Self-sufficiency fatal to the family.—The shortcoming which most frequently keeps individuals outside of the family, and keeps them incomplete and imperfect members of the family after they enter it, is the self-sufficiency which is induced by a life of protracted independence. Marriage is from one point of view a sacrifice, a giving-up. The bachelor can spend more money on himself than can the married man who must provide for wife and children. The single woman can give to study and music and travel an amount of time and attention which is impossible to the wife and mother. Such a view of marriage is supremely mean and selfish. Only a very little and sordid soul could entertain it. There are often the best and noblest of reasons why man or woman should remain single. It is a duty to do so rather than to marry from any motive save purest love. Marriage, however, should be regarded as the ideal state for every man and [154]woman. To refuse to marry for merely selfish reasons; or to carry over into marriage the selfish individualistic temper, which clings so tenaciously to the little individual self that it can never attain the larger self which comes from real union and devotion to another—this is to sin against human nature, and to prove one's self unworthy of membership in society's most fundamental and sacred institution.

The child who sets his own will against his parent's, the mother who thrusts her child out of her presence in order to pursue pleasures more congenial than the nurture of her own offspring, the man who leaves his family night after night to spend his evenings in the club or the saloon, the woman who spends on dress and society the money that is needed to relieve her husband from overwork and anxiety, and to bring up her children in health and intelligence, do an irreparable wrong to the family, and deal a death blow to the home.

THE VICE OF EXCESS.

Self-obliteration robs the family of the best we have to give it.—The man who makes himself a slave; goes beyond his strength; denies himself needed rest and recreation; grows prematurely old, cuts himself off from intercourse with his fellow-men in order to secure for his family a position or a fortune: the woman who works early and late; forgets her music, and forsakes her favorite books; gives up friends and society; grows anxious and careworn in [155]order to give her sons and daughters a better start in life than she had, are making a fatal mistake. In the effort to provide their children with material things and intellectual advantages they are depriving them of what even to the children is of far more consequence—healthy, happy, cheerful, interesting, enthusiastic parents. To their children as well as to themselves parents owe it to be the brightest, cheeriest, heartiest, wisest, completest persons that they are capable of being. Children also when they have reached maturity, although they owe to their parents a reverent regard for all reasonable desires and wishes, ought not to sacrifice opportunities for gaining a desired education or an advantageous start in business, merely to gratify a capricious whim or groundless foreboding of an arbitrary and unreasoning parent. Devotion to the family does not imply withdrawal from the world outside. The larger and fuller one's relations to the world without, the deeper and richer ought to be one's contribution to the family of which he is a member.

THE PENALTY.

To have no one for whom we supremely care, and no one who cares much for us; to have no place where we can shield ourselves from outward opposition and inward despair; to have no larger life in which we can merge the littleness of our solitary selves; to touch other lives only on the surface, and to take no one to our heart;—this is the sad estate of the man or [156]woman who refuses to enter with whole-souled devotion into union with another in the building of a family and a home.—The sense that this loneliness is chosen in fidelity to duty makes it endurable for multitudes of noble men and women. But for the man or woman who chooses such a life in proud self-sufficiency, for the sake of fancied freedom and independence, it is hard to conceive what consolation can be found. Thomas Carlyle, speaking of the joys of living in close union with those who love us, and whom we love, says: "It is beautiful; it is human! Man lives not otherwise, nor can live contented, anywhere or anywhen. Isolation is the sum-total of wretchedness to man. To be cut off, to be left solitary; to have a world alien, not your world; all a hostile camp for you; not a home at all, of hearts and faces who are yours, whose you are! It is the frightfullest enchantment; too truly a work of the Evil One. To have neither superior, nor inferior, nor equal, united manlike to you. Without father, without child, without brother. Man knows no sadder destiny."

[157]

CHAPTER XIX.

The State.

Out of the family grew the state. The primitive state was an enlarged family, of which the father was the head. Citizenship meant kinship, real or fictitious. The house or gens was a composite family. Houses united into tribes, and the authority of the chieftain over his fellow-tribesmen was still based on the fact that they were, either by birthright or adoption, his children. The ancient state was the union of tribes under one priest and king who was regarded as the father of the whole people.

Disputes about the right of succession, and the disadvantage and danger of having a tyrant or a weakling rule, just because he happened to be the son of the previous ruler, led men to elect their rulers. There are to-day states like Russia where the hereditary monarch is the ruler: states like the United States where all rulers are elected by the people; and states like England where the nominal ruler is an hereditary monarch, and the real rulers are chosen by the people.

THE DUTY.

The function of the state is the organization of the life of the people.—Men can live together in [158]peace and happiness only on condition that they assert for themselves and respect in others certain rights to life, liberty, property, reputation, and opinion. My right it is my neighbor's duty to observe. His right it is my duty to respect. These mutual rights and duties are grounded in the nature of things and the constitution of man. They are the conditions which must be observed if man is to live in unity with his fellow-men. It is the business of the state to define, declare, and enforce these rights and duties. And as citizens it is our duty to the state to do all in our power to frame just laws; to see that they are impartially and effectively administered; to obey these laws ourselves; to contribute our share of the funds necessary to maintain the government; and to render military service when force is needed to protect the government from overthrow. To law and government we owe all that makes life endurable or even possible: the security of property; the sanctity of home; the opportunity of education; the stability of institutions; the blessings of peace; protection against violence and bloodshed. Since the state and its laws are essential to the well-being of all men, and consequently of ourselves; we owe to it the devotion of our time, our knowledge, our influence, yes, our life itself if need be. If it comes to a choice between living but a brief time, and that nobly, in devotion to country, and living a long time basely, in betrayal of our country's good, no true, brave man will hesitate to choose the former. In times of war and revolution that choice [159]has been presented to men in every age and country: and men have always been found ready to choose the better part; death for country, rather than life apart from her. So deep was the conviction in the mind of Socrates that the laws of the state should be obeyed at all costs, that when he had been sentenced to death unjustly, and had an opportunity to escape the penalty by running away, he refused to do it on the ground that it was his duty to obey those laws which had made him what he was and whose protection he had enjoyed so many years. To the friend who tried to induce him to escape he replied that he seemed to hear the laws saying to him, "Our country is more to be valued and higher and holier far than father or mother. And when we are punished by her, whether with imprisonment or stripes, the punishment is to be endured in silence; and if she sends us to wounds or death in battle, thither we follow as is right; neither may anyone yield or retreat or leave his rank, but whether in battle or in a court of law, or in any other place, he must do what his city and his country order him; or he must change their view of what is just; and if he may do no violence to his father or mother, much less may he do violence to his country." To do and bear whatever is necessary to maintain that organization of life which the state represents is the imperative duty of every citizen. This duty to serve the country is correlative to the right to be a citizen. No man can be in truth and spirit a citizen on any other terms. And not to be a citizen [160]is not to be, in any true and worthy meaning of the term, a man.

THE VIRTUE.

Love of country, or patriotism, like all love places the object loved first and self second.—In all public action the patriot asks not, "What is best for me?" but, "What is best for my country?" Patriotism assumes as many forms as there are circumstances and ways in which the welfare of the country may be promoted. In time of war the patriot shoulders his gun and marches to fight the enemy. In time of election he goes to the caucus and the polls, and expresses his opinion and casts his vote for what he believes to be just measures and honest men. When taxes are to be levied, he gives the assessor a full account of his property, and pays his fair share of the expense of government. When one party proposes measures and nominates men whom he considers better than those of the opposite party, he votes with that party, whether it is for his private interest to do so or not. The patriot will not stand apart from all parties, because none is good enough for him. He will choose the best, knowing that no political party is perfect. He will act with that party as long as it continues to seem to him the best; for he must recognize that one man standing alone can accomplish no practical political result. The moment he is convinced that the party with which he has been acting has become more corrupt, and less faithful to the interests of [161]the country than the opposite party, he will change his vote. Self first, personal friends second, party third, and country fourth, is the order of considerations in the mind of the office-seeker, the wire-puller, the corrupt politician. Country first, party second, personal friends third, and self last is the order in the mind of the true citizen, the courageous statesman, the unselfish patriot.

THE REWARD.

In return for serving our country we receive a country to serve.—The state makes possible for us all those pursuits, interests, aims, and aspirations which lift our lives above the level of the brutes. Through the institutions which the state maintains, schools, almshouses, courts, prisons, roads, bridges, harbors, laws, armies, police, there is secured to the individual the right and opportunity to acquire property, engage in business, travel wherever he pleases, share in the products of the whole earth, read the books of all nations, reap the fruits of scholarly investigation in all countries, take an interest in the welfare and progress of mankind. This power of the individual to live a universal life, this participation of each in a common and world-wide good, is the product of civilization. And civilization is impossible without that subordination of each to the just claims of all, which law requires and which it is the business of the state to enforce.

[162] THE TEMPTATION.

Organization involves a multitude of offices and public servants. Many of these offices are less onerous and more lucrative than the average man can find elsewhere. Many offices give a man an opportunity to acquire dishonest gains.—Hence arises the great political temptation which is to seek office, not as a means of rendering useful and honorable service to the country, but as a means to getting an easy living out of the country, and at the public expense. The "spoils system," which consists in rewarding service to party by opportunity to plunder the country: which pays public servants first for their service to party, and secondly for service to the country: which makes usefulness to party rather than serviceableness to the country the basis of appointment and promotion, is the worst evil of our political life. "Public office is a public trust." Men who so regard it are the only men fit for it. Office so held is one of the most honorable forms of service which a man can render to his fellow-men. Office secured and held by the methods of the spoils system is a disgrace to the nation that is corrupt enough to permit it, and to the man who is base enough to profit by it.

THE VICE OF DEFECT.

Betrayal of one's country and disregard of its interests is treason.—In time of war and revolution treason consists in giving information to the [163]enemy, surrendering forts, ships, arms, or ammunition into his hands; or fighting in such a half-hearted way as to invite defeat. Treason under such circumstances is the unpardonable sin against country. The traitor is the most despicable person in the state; for he takes advantage of the protection the state gives to him and the confidence it places in him to stab and murder his benefactor and protector.

The essential quality of treason is manifested in many forms in time of peace. Whoever sacrifices the known interests of his country to the interests of himself, or of his friends, or of his party, is therein guilty of the essential crime of treason. Whoever votes for an appropriation in order to secure for another man lucrative employment or a profitable contract; whoever gives or takes money for a vote; whoever increases or diminishes a tax with a view to the business interests, not of the country as a whole, but of a few interested parties; whoever accepts or bestows a public office on any grounds other than the efficiency of service which the office-holder is to render to the country; whoever evades his just taxes; whoever suffers bad men to be elected and bad measures to become laws through his own negligence to vote himself and to influence others to vote for better men and better measures, is guilty of treason. For in these, which are the only ways possible to him, he has sacrificed the good of his country to the personal and private interests of himself and of his friends.

[164] THE VICE OF EXCESS.

True and false ambition.—The service of the country in public office is one of the most interesting and most honorable pursuits in which a man can engage. Ambition to serve is always noble. Desire for the honors and emoluments of public office, however, may crowd out the desire to render public service. Such a substitution of selfish for patriotic considerations, such an inversion of the proper order of interests in a man's mind, is the vice of political ambition. The ambitious politician seeks office, not because he seeks to promote measures which he believes to be for the public good; not because he believes he can promote those interests more effectively than any other available candidate: but just because an office makes him feel big; or because he likes the excitement of political life; or because he can make money directly or indirectly out of it. Such political ambition is as hollow and empty an aim as can possess the mind of man. And yet it deceives and betrays great as well as little men. It is our old foe of sentimentality, dressed in a new garb, and displaying itself on a new stage. It is the substitution of one's own personal feelings, for a direct regard for the object which makes those feelings possible. It is a very subtle vice: and the only safeguard against it is a deep and genuine devotion to country for country's sake.

[165] THE PENALTY.

A state in which laws were broken, taxes evaded, and corrupt men placed in authority could not endure.—With the downfall of the state would arise the brigand, the thief, the murderer, and the reign of dishonesty, violence, and terror.

The individual, it is true, may sin against the state and escape the full measure of this penalty himself. In that case, however, the penalty is distributed over the vast multitude of honest citizens, who bear the common injury which the traitor inflicts upon the state. The man who betrays his country, may continue to have a country still; but it is no thanks to him. It is because he reaps the reward of the loyalty and devotion of citizens nobler than himself.

Yet even then the country is not in the deepest sense really his. He cannot enjoy its deepest blessings. He cannot feel in his inmost heart, "This country is mine. To it I have given myself. Of it I am a true citizen and loyal member." He knows he is unworthy of his country. He knows that if his country could find him out, and separate him from the great mass of his fellow-citizens, she would repudiate him as unworthy to be called her son. The traitor may continue to receive the gifts of his country; he may appropriate the blessings she bestows with impartial hand on the good and on the evil. But the sense that this glorious and righteous order of which the state is the embodiment and of which [166]our country is the preserver and protector belongs to him; that it is an expression of his thought, his will and his affection;—this spiritual participation in the life and spirit of the state, this supreme devotion to a beloved country, remains for such an one forever impossible. In his soul, in his real nature, he is an outcast, an alien, and an enemy.

[167]

CHAPTER XX.

Society.

Regard for others, merely as individuals, does not satisfy the deepest yearnings of our social nature. The family is so much more to us than the closest of ties which we can form on lines of business, charity, or even friendship; because in place of an aggregate of individuals, each with his separate interests, the family presents a life in which each member shares in a good which is common to all.

The state makes possible a common good on a much wider scale. Still, on a strict construction of its functions, the state merely insures the outward form of this wider, common life. The state declares what man shall not do, rather than what man shall do, in his relations to his fellow-men. To prevent the violation of mutual rights rather than to secure the performance of mutual duties, is the fundamental function of the state. Of course these two sides cannot be kept entirely apart. There is a strong tendency at the present time to enlarge the province of the state, and to intrust it with the enforcement of positive duties which man owes to his fellow-men, and which class owes to class. Whether this tendency is good or bad, whether it is desirable to enforce social duties, or to trust them [168]to the unfettered social conscience of mankind, is a theoretical question which, for our practical purposes, we need not here discuss.

No man liveth unto himself. No man ought to be satisfied with a good which is peculiar to himself, from which mankind as a whole are excluded. No man can be so satisfied. Ignorance, prejudice, selfishness, pride, custom, blind men to this common good, and prevent them from making the efforts and sacrifices necessary to realize it. But the man who could deliberately prefer to see the world in which he lives going to destruction would be a monster rather than a man.

This common life of humanity in which each individual partakes is society. Society is the larger self of each individual. Its interests and ours are fundamentally one and the same.—If the society in which we live is elevated and pure and noble we share its nobleness and are elevated by it. If society is low, corrupt, and degraded, we share its corruption, and its baseness drags us down. So vital and intimate is this bond between society and ourselves that it is impossible when dealing with moral matters to keep them apart. To be a better man, without at the same time being a better neighbor, citizen, workman, soldier, scholar, or business man, is a contradiction in terms. For life consists in these social relations to our fellows. And the better we are, the better these social duties will be fulfilled.

Society includes all the objects hitherto [169]considered. Society is the organic life of man, in which the particular objects and relations of our individual lives are elements and members. Hence in this chapter, and throughout the remainder of the book, we shall not be concerned with new materials, but with the materials with which we are already familiar, viewed in their broader and more comprehensive relationships.

THE DUTY.

In each act we should think not merely "How will this act affect me?" but "How will this act affect all parties concerned, and society as a whole?"—The interests of all men are my own, by virtue of that common society of which they and I are equal members. What is good for others is good for me, because, in that broader view of my own nature which society embodies, my good cannot be complete unless, to the extent of my ability, their good is included in my own. Hence we have the maxims laid down by Kant: "Act as if the maxim of thy action were to become by thy will a universal law of nature." "So act as to treat humanity, whether in thine own person or in that of another, in every case as an end, never as a means only." Or as Professor Royce puts the same thought; "Act as a being would act who included thy will and thy neighbor's will in the unity of one life, and who had therefore to suffer the consequences for the aims of both that will follow from the act of either." "In so far as in thee lies, act as if thou [170]wert at once thy neighbor and thyself. Treat these two lives as one."

The realization of the good of all in and through the act of each is the social ideal.—In everyday matters this can be brought about by simply taking account of all the interests of others which will be affected by our act. In the relations between employer and employee, for instance, profit sharing is the most practical form of realizing this community of interest. Such action involves a co-operation of interests as the motives of the individual act.

The larger social ends, such as education, philanthropy, reform, public improvements, require the co-operation of many individuals in the same enterprise. The readiness to contribute a fair share of our time, money, and influence to these larger public interests, which no individual can undertake alone, is an important part of our social duty. Every beneficent cause, every effort to rouse public sentiment against a wrong, or to make it effective in the enforcement of a right; every endeavor to unite men in social intercourse; every plan to extend the opportunities for education; every measure for the relief of the deserving poor, and the protection of homeless children; every wise movement for the prevention of vice, crime, and intemperance, is entitled to receive from each one of us the same intelligent attention, the same keenness of interest, the same energy of devotion, the same sacrifice of inclination and convenience, the same resoluteness [171]and courage of action that we give to our private affairs.

Co-operation, then, is of two kinds, inward and outward: co-operation between the interests of others and of ourselves in the motive to our individual action; and co-operation of our action with the action of others to accomplish objects too vast for private undertaking.—Both forms of co-operation are in principle the same; they strengthen and support each other. The man who is in the habit of considering the interests of others in his individual acts will be more ready to unite with others in the promotion of public beneficence. And on the other hand the man who is accustomed to act with others in large public movements will be more inclined to act for others in his personal affairs. The reformer and philanthropist is simply the man of private generosity and good-will acting out his nature on a larger stage.

THE VIRTUE.

Public spirit is the life of the community in the heart of the individual.—This recognition that we belong to society, and that society belongs to us, that its interests are our interests, that its wrongs are ours to redress, its rights are ours to maintain, its losses are ours to bear, its blessings are ours to enjoy, is public spirit.

A generous regard for the public welfare, a willingness to lend a hand in any movement for the improvement of social conditions, a readiness with [172]work and influence and time and money to relieve suffering, improve sanitary conditions, promote education and morality, remove temptation from the weak, open reading-rooms and places of harmless resort for the unoccupied in their evening hours, to bind together persons of similar tastes and pursuits—these are the marks of public spirit; these are the manifestations of social virtue.

Politeness is love in little things.—Toward individuals whom we meet in social ways this recognition of our common nature and mutual rights takes the form of politeness and courtesy. Politeness is proper respect for human personality. Rudeness results from thinking exclusively about ourselves, and caring nothing for the feelings of anybody else. The sincere and generous desire to bring the greatest pleasure and the least pain to everyone we meet will go a long way toward making our manners polite and courteous.

Still, society has agreed upon certain more or less arbitrary ways for facilitating social intercourse; it has established rules for conduct on social occasions, and to a certain extent prescribed the forms of words that shall be used, the modes of salutation that shall be employed, the style of dress that shall be worn, and the like. A due respect for society, and for the persons whom we meet socially, demands that we shall acquaint ourselves with these rules of etiquette, and observe them in our social intercourse. Like all forms, social formalities are easily carried to excess, and frequently kill the spirit they [173]are intended to express. As a basis, however, for the formation of acquaintances, and for large social gatherings, a good deal of formality is necessary.

THE REWARD.

The complete expression and outgo of our nature is freedom.—Since man is by nature social, since sympathy, friendship, co-operation and affection are essential attributes of man, it follows that the exercise of these social virtues is itself the satisfaction of what is essentially ourselves.

The man who fulfills his social duties is free, for he finds an open field and an unfettered career for the most essential faculties of his nature. The social man always has friends whom he loves; work which he feels to be worth doing; interests which occupy his highest powers; causes which appeal to his deepest sympathies. Such a life of rounded activity, of arduous endeavor, of full, free self-expression is in itself the highest possible reward. It is the only form of satisfaction worthy of man. It is in the deepest sense of the word success. For as Lowell says:

All true whole men succeed, for what is worthSuccess's name, unless it be the thought,The inward surety to have carried outA noble purpose to a noble end.

THE TEMPTATION.

Instead of regarding society as a whole, and self as a member of that whole, it is possible to regard self as distinct and separate from society, [174]and to make the interests of this separated and detached self the end and aim of action.—This temptation is self-interest. It consists in placing the individual self, with its petty, private, personal interests, above the social self, with the large, public, generous interests of the social order.

From one point of view it is easy to cheat society, and deprive it of its due. We can shirk our social obligations; we can dodge subscriptions; we can stay at home when we ought to be at the committee meeting, or the public gathering; we can decline invitations and refuse elections to arduous offices, and at the same time escape many of the worst penalties which would naturally follow from our neglect. For others, more generous and noble than we, will step in and take upon themselves our share of the public burdens in addition to their own. We may flatter ourselves that we have done a very shrewd thing in contriving to reap the benefits without bearing the burdens of society. There is, as we shall see, a penalty for negligence of social duty, and that too most sure and terrible. Self-interest is the seed, of which meanness is the full-grown plant, and of which social constraint and slavishness are the final fruits.

THE VICE OF DEFECT.

Lack of public spirit is meanness.—The mean man is he who acknowledges no interest and recognizes no obligation outside the narrow range of his strictly private concerns. As long as he is comfortable [175]he will take no steps to relieve the distress of others. If his own premises are healthy, he will contribute nothing to improve the sanitary condition of his village or city. As long as his own property is secure he cares not how many criminals are growing up in the street, how many are sent to prison, or how they are treated after they come there. He favors the cheapest schools, the poorest roads, the plainest public buildings, because he would rather keep his money in his own pocket than contribute his share to maintain a thoroughly efficient and creditable public service. He will give nothing he can help giving, do nothing he can help doing, to make the town he lives in a healthier, happier, purer, wiser, nobler place. Meanness is the sacrifice of the great social whole to the individual. It is selfishness, stinginess, and ingratitude combined. It is the disposition to receive all that society contributes to the individual, and to give nothing in return. It is a willingness to appropriate the fruits of labors in which one refuses to bear a part.

THE VICE OF EXCESS.

The officious person is ready for any and every kind of public service, providing he can be at the head of it. There is no end to the work he will do if he can only have his own way.—He wants to be prime mover in every enterprise: to be chairman of the committee; to settle every question that comes up; to "run" things according to his own ideas. Such people are often very useful. It is [176]generally wisest not to meddle much with them. The work may not be done in the best way by these officious people; but without them a great deal of public work would never be done at all. The vice, however, seriously impairs one's usefulness. The officious person is hard to work with. Men refuse to have anything to do with him. And so he is left to do his work for the most part alone. Officiousness is, in reality, social ambition; and that again as we saw resolves itself into sentimentality;—the regard for what we and others think of ourselves, rather than straightforward devotion to the ends which we pretend to be endeavoring to promote. Officiousness is self-seeking dressed up in the uniform of service. The officious person, instead of losing his private self in the larger life of society, tries to use the larger interests of society in such a way as to make them gratify his own personal vanity and sense of self-importance.

THE PENALTY.

All meanness and self-seeking are punished by lack of freedom or constraint; though frequently the constraint is inward and spiritual rather than outward and physical.—We have seen that to the man of generous public spirit society presents a career for the unfolding and expansion of his social powers. To such a man society, with its claims and obligations, is an enlargement of his range of sympathy, a widening of his spiritual horizon, and on [177]that account a means of larger liberty and fuller freedom.

To the mean and selfish man, on the contrary, society presents itself as an alien force, a hard task-master, making severe requirements upon his time, imposing cramping limitations on his self-indulgence, levying heavy taxes upon his substance; prescribing onerous rules and regulations for his conduct.

By excluding society from the sphere of interests with which he identifies himself, the mean man, by his own meanness, makes society antagonistic to him, and himself its reluctant and unwilling slave. Serve it to some extent he must; but the selfishness and meanness of his own attitude toward it, makes social service, not the willing and joyous offering of a free and devoted heart, but the slavish submission of a reluctant will, forced to do the little that it cannot help doing by legal or social compulsion.

To him society is not a sphere of freedom, in which his own nature is enlarged, intensified, liberated; and so made richer, happier, nobler, and freer. To him society is an external power, compelling him to make sacrifices he does not want to make; to do things he does not want to do; to contribute money which he grudges, and to conform to requirements which he hates. By trying to save the life of self-interest and meanness, he loses the life of generous aims, noble ideals, and heroic self devotion.

By refusing the career of noble freedom which [178]social service offers to each member of the social body, he is constrained to obey a social law which he has not helped to create, and to serve the interests of a society of which he has refused to be in spirit and truth a part.

This living in a world which we do not heartily acknowledge as our own; this subjection to an authority which we do not in principle recognize and welcome as the voice of our own better, larger, wiser, social self,—this is constraint and slavery in its basest and most degrading form.

---

[179]

CHAPTER XXI.

Self.

Hitherto we have considered things, relations, persons, and institutions outside ourselves as the objects which together constitute our environment.

The self is not a new object, but rather the bond which binds together into unity all the experiences of life. It is their relation to this conscious self which gives to all objects their moral worth. Every act upon an object reacts upon ourselves. The virtues and vices, the rewards and penalties that we have been studying are the various reactions of conduct upon ourselves. This chapter then will be a comprehensive review and summary of all that has gone before. Instead of taking one by one the particular reactions which follow particular acts with reference to particular objects, we shall now look at conduct as a whole; regard our environment in its totality; and consider duty, virtue, and self in their unity.

THE DUTY.

The duty we owe to ourselves is the realization of our capacities and powers in harmony with each other, and in proportion to their worth as elements in a complete individual and social life.—We have within us the capacity for an ever [180]increasing fullness and richness and intensity of life. The materials out of which this life is to be developed are ready to our hands in those objects which we have been considering. One way of conduct toward these objects, which we have called duty; one attitude of mind and will toward them which we have called virtue, leads to those completions and fulfillments of ourselves which we have called rewards. Duty then to self; duty in its most comprehensive aspect, is the obligation which the existence of capacity within and material without imposes on us to bring the two together in harmonious relations, so as to realize the capacities and powers of ourselves and of others, and promote society's well being. In simpler terms our fundamental duty is to make the most of ourselves; and to become as large and genuine a part of the social world in which we live as it is possible for us to be.

THE VIRTUE.

The habit of seeking to realize the highest capacities and widest relationships of our nature in every act is conscientiousness. Conscience is our consciousness of the ideal in conduct and character. Conscience is the knowledge of our duty, coupled as that knowledge always is with the feeling that we ought to do it.—

Knowledge of any kind calls up some feeling appropriate to the fact known. Knowledge that a given act would realize my ideal calls up the feeling of dissatisfaction with myself until that act is [181]performed; because that is the feeling appropriate to the recognition of an unrealized yet attainable ideal. Conscience is not a mysterious faculty of our nature. It is simply thought and feeling, recognizing and responding to the fact of duty, and reaching out toward virtue and excellence.

The objective worth of the deliverances and dictates of the conscience of the individual, depends on the degree of moral enlightenment and sensitiveness he has attained. The conscience of an educated Christian has a worth and authority which the conscience of the benighted savage has not. Since conscience is the recognition of the ideal of conduct and character, every new appreciation of duty and virtue gives to conscience added strength and clearness.

The absolute authority of conscience.—Relatively to the individual himself, at the time of acting, his own individual conscience is the final and absolute authority. The man who does what his conscience tells him, does the best that he can do. For he realizes the highest ideal that is present to his mind. A wiser man than he might do better than this man, acting according to his conscience, is able to do. But this man, with the limited knowledge and imperfect ideal which he actually has, can do no more than obey his conscience which bids him realize the highest ideal that he knows. The act of the conscientious man may be right or wrong, judged by objective, social standards. Judged by subjective standards, seen from within, every [182]conscientious act is, relatively to the individual himself, a right act. We should spare no pains to enlighten our conscience, and make it the reflection of the most exalted ideals which society has reached. Having done this, conscience becomes to us the authoritative judge for us of what we shall, and what we shall not do. The light of conscience will be clear and pure, or dim and clouded, according to the completeness of our moral environment, training, and insight. But clear or dim, high or low, sensitive or dull, the light of conscience is the only light we have to guide us in the path of virtue. In hours of leisure and study it is our privilege to inform and clarify this consciousness of the ideal. That has been the purpose of the preceding pages. When the time for action comes, then, without a murmur, without an instant's hesitation, the voice of conscience should be implicitly obeyed. Conscientiousness is the form which all the virtues take, when viewed as determinations of the self. It is the assertion of the ideal of the self in its every act.

THE REWARD.

Character the form in which the result of virtuous conduct is preserved.—It is neither possible nor desirable to solve each question of conduct as it arises by conscious and explicit reference to rules and principles. Were we to attempt to do so it would make us prigs and prudes.

What then is the use of studying at such length the temptations and duties, the virtues and vices, [183]with their rewards and penalties, if all these things are to be forgotten and ignored when the occasions for practical action arrive?

The study of ethics has the same use as the study of writing, grammar, or piano-playing. In learning to write we have to think precisely how each letter is formed, how one letter is connected with another, where to use capitals, where to punctuate and the like. But after we have become proficient in writing, we do all this without once thinking explicitly of any of these things. In learning to play the piano we have to count out loud in order to keep time correctly, and we are obliged to stop and think just where to put the finger in order to strike each separate note. But the expert player does all these things without the slightest conscious effort.

Still, though the particular rules and principles are not consciously present in each act of the finished writer or musician, they are not entirely absent. When the master of these arts makes a mistake, he recognizes it instantly, and corrects it, or endeavors to avoid its repetition. This shows that the rule is not lost. It has ceased to be before the mind as a distinct object of consciousness. It is no longer needed in that form for ordinary purposes. Instead, it has come to be a part of the mind itself—a way in which the mind works instinctively. As long as the mind works in conformity with the principle, it is not distinctly recognized, because there is no need for such recognition. The principle [184]comes to consciousness only as a power to check or restrain acts that are at variance with it.

It is in this way that the practical man carries with him his ethical principles. He does not stop to reason out the relation of duty and virtue to reward, or of temptation and vice to penalty, before he decides to help the unfortunate, or to be faithful to a friend, or to vote on election day. This trained, habitual will, causing acts to be performed in conformity to duty and virtue, yet without conscious reference to the explicit principles that underlie them, is character.

It is chiefly in the formation of character that the explicit recognition of ethical principles has its value. Character is a storage battery in which the power acquired by our past acts is accumulated and preserved for future use.

It is through this power of character, this tendency of acts of a given nature to repeat and perpetuate themselves, that we give unity and consistency to our lives. This also is the secret of our power of growth. As soon as one virtue has become habitual and enters into our character, we can leave it, trusting it in the hands of this unconscious power of self-perpetuation; and then we can turn the energy thus freed toward the acquisition of new virtues.

Day by day we are turning over more and more of our lives to this domain of character. Hence it is of the utmost importance to allow nothing to enter this almost irrevocable state of unconscious, habitual character that has not first received the [185]approval of conscience, the sanction of duty, and the stamp of virtue. Character, once formed in a wrong direction, may be corrected. But it can be done only with the greatest difficulty, and by a process as hard to resolve upon as the amputation of a limb or the plucking out of an eye.

The greater part of the principles of ethics we knew before we undertook this formal study. We learned them from our parents; we picked them up in contact with one another in the daily intercourse of life. The value of our study will not consist so much in new truths learned, as in the clearer and sharper outlines which it will have given to some of the features of the moral ideal. The definite results of such a study we cannot mark or measure. Just as sunshine and rain come to the plants and trees, and then seem to vanish, leaving no visible or tangible trace behind; yet the plants and trees are different from what they were before, and have the heat and moisture stored up within their structure to burst forth into fresher and larger life; in like manner, though we should forget every formal statement that we have read, yet we could not fail to be affected by the incorporation within ourselves in the form of character of some of these principles of duty and virtue which we have been considering. It has been said: "Sow an act, and you reap a habit; sow a habit and you reap a character; sow a character and you reap a destiny."

[186] THE TEMPTATION.

Pleasure not a reliable guide to conduct.—The realization of capacity brings with it pleasure. The harmonious realization of all our powers would bring harmonious and permanent pleasure or happiness. Pleasure is always to be welcomed as a sign of health and activity. Other things being equal, the more pleasure we have the better. It is possible however to abstract the pleasure from the activity which gives rise to it, and make pleasure the end for which we act. This pursuit of pleasure for pleasure's sake is delusive and destructive. It is delusive, because the direct aim at pleasure turns us aside from the direct aim at objects. And when we cease to aim directly at objects, we begin to lose the pleasure and zest which only a direct pursuit of objects can produce. For instance, we all know that if we go to a picnic or a party thinking all the while about having a good time, and asking ourselves every now and then whether we are having a good time or not, we find the picnic or party a dreadful bore, and ourselves perfectly miserable. We know that the whole secret of having a good time on such occasions is to get interested in something else; a game, a boat-ride, anything that makes us forget ourselves and our pleasures, and helps us to lose ourselves in the eager, arduous, absorbing pursuit of something outside ourselves. Then we have a glorious time.

The direct pursuit of pleasure is destructive of character, because it judges things by the way they [187]affect our personal feelings; which is a very shallow and selfish standard of judgment; and because it centers interest in the merely emotional side of our nature, which is peculiar to ourselves; instead of in the rational part of our nature which is common to all men, and unites us to our fellows.

Duty demands not the hap-hazard realization of this or that side of our nature. Yet this is what the pursuit of pleasure would lead to. Duty demands the realization of all our faculties, in harmony with each other, and in proportion to their worth. And to this proportioned and harmonious realization, pleasure, pure and simple, is no guide at all. Hence, as Aristotle remarks, "In all cases we must be specially on our guard against pleasant things and against pleasure: for we can scarce judge her impartially." "Again, as the exercises of our faculties differ in goodness and badness, and some are to be desired and some to be shunned, so do the several pleasures differ; for each exercise has its proper pleasure. The pleasure which is proper to a good activity, then, is good, and that which is proper to one that is not good is bad." "As the exercises of the faculties vary, so do their respective pleasures."

To the same effect John Stuart Mill says that the pleasures which result from the exercise of the higher faculties are to be preferred. "It is better to be a human being dissatisfied, than a pig satisfied; better to be Socrates dissatisfied than a fool satisfied." Whether it is possible to stretch, and qualify, and attenuate the conception of pleasure so as to [188]make it cover the ideal of human life, without having it, like a soap-bubble, burst in the process, is a question foreign to the practical purpose of this book. That pleasure, as ordinarily understood by plain people, is a treacherous, dangerous, and ruinous guide to conduct, moralists of every school declare. Pleasure is the most subtle and universal form of temptation. Pleasure is the accompaniment of all exercise of power. When it comes rightly it is to be accepted with thankfulness. We must remember however that the quality of the act determines the worth of the pleasure; and that the amount of pleasure does not determine the quality of the act. A pleasant act may be right, and it may be wrong. Whether we ought to do it or not must in every case be decided on higher grounds.

To the boy who says, "I should like to be something that would make me a great man, and very happy besides—something that would not hinder me from having a great deal of pleasure"—George Eliot represents "Romola" as replying, "That is not easy, my Lillo. It is only a poor sort of happiness that could ever come by caring very much about our own narrow pleasures. We can only have the highest happiness, such as goes along with being a great man, by having wide thoughts, and much feeling for the rest of the world as well as for ourselves; and this sort of happiness often brings so much pain with it that we can only tell it from pain by its being what we would choose before everything else, because our souls see it is good. And so, my Lillo, [189]if you mean to act nobly and seek to know the best things God has put within reach of men, you must learn to fix your mind on that end, and not on what will happen to you because of it. And remember, if you were to choose something lower, and make it the rule of your life to seek your own pleasure and escape from what is disagreeable, calamity might come just the same; and it would be calamity falling on a base mind, which is the one form of sorrow that has no balm in it, and that may well make a man say—It would have been better for me if I had never been born."

THE VICE OF DEFECT.

The unscrupulous man acts as he happens to feel like acting.— Whatever course of conduct presents itself as pleasant, or profitable, or easy, he adopts. Anything is good enough for him. He seeks to embody no ideal, aims consistently at no worthy end, acknowledges no duty, but simply yields himself a passive instrument for lust, or avarice, or cowardice, or falsehood to play upon. Refusing to be the servant of virtue he becomes the slave of vice. Disowning the authority of duty and the ideal, he becomes the tool of appetite, the football of circumstance. Unscrupulousness is the form of all the vices of defect, when viewed in relation to that absence of regard for realization of self, which is their common characteristic.

[190] THE VICE OF EXCESS.

The exclusive regard for self, in abstraction from those objects and social relationships through which alone the self can be truly realized, leads to formalism.—Formalism keeps the law simply for the sake of keeping it. Conscientiousness, if it is wise and well-balanced, reverences the duties and requirements of the moral life, because these duties are the essential conditions of individual and social well-being. The law is a means to well-being, which is the end. Formalism makes the law an end in itself; and will even sacrifice well-being to law, when the two squarely conflict.

Extreme cases in which moral laws may be suspended.—The particular duties, virtues, and laws which society has established and recognized are the expressions of reason and experience declaring the conditions of human well-being. As such they deserve our profoundest respect; our unswerving obedience. Still it is impossible for rules to cover every case. There are legitimate, though very rare, exceptions, even to moral laws and duties. For instance it is a duty to respect the property of others. Yet to save the life of a person who is starving, we are justified in taking the property of another without asking his consent. To save a person from drowning, we may seize a boat belonging to another. To spread the news of a fire, we may take the first horse we find, without inquiring who is the owner. To save a sick person from a fatal [191] shock, we may withhold facts in violation of the strict duty of truthfulness. To promote an important public measure, we may deliberately break down our health, spend our private fortune, and reduce ourselves to helpless beggary. Such acts violate particular duties. They break moral laws. And yet they all are justified in these extreme cases by the higher law of love; by the greater duty of devotion to the highest good of our fellow-men. The doctrine that "the end justifies the means" is a mischievous and dangerous doctrine. Stated in that unqualified form, it is easily made the excuse for all sorts of immorality. The true solution of the seeming conflict of duties lies in the recognition that the larger social good justifies the sacrifice of the lesser social good when the two conflict. One must remember, however, that the universal recognition of established duties and laws is itself the greatest social good; and only the most extreme cases can justify a departure from the path of generally recognized and established moral law.

These extreme cases when they occur, however, must be dealt with bravely. The form of law and rule must be sacrificed to the substance of righteousness and love when the two conflict. As Professor Marshall remarks in the chapter of his "History of Greek Philosophy" which deals with Socrates, "The highest activity does not always take the form of conformity to rule. There are critical moments when rules fail, when, in fact, obedience to rule would mean disobedience to that higher law, of [192]which rules and formulæ are at best only an adumbration."

There is nothing more contemptible than that timid, self-seeking virtue which will sacrifice the obvious well-being of others to save itself the pain of breaking a rule. There is nothing more pitiful than that self-righteous virtue which does right, not because it loves the right, still less because it loves the person who is affected by its action, but simply because it wants to keep its own sweet sense of self-righteousness unimpaired. Mrs. Browning gives us a clear example of this "harmless life, she called a virtuous life," in the case of the frigid aunt of "Aurora Leigh":

From that day, she didHer duty to me (I appreciate itIn her own word as spoken to herself),Her duty, in large measure, well-pressed out,But measured always. She was generous, bland,More courteous than was tender, gave me stillThe first place,—as if fearful that God's saintsWould look down suddenly and say, 'HereinYou missed a point, I think, through lack of love.'

THE PENALTY.

Just as continuity in virtue strengthens and unifies character and makes life a consistent and harmonious whole; so self-indulgence in vicious pleasures disorganizes a man's life and eats the heart out of him.—Corrupt means literally broken. The corrupt man has no soundness, no solidity, no unity in his life. He cannot respect himself. [193]Others cannot put confidence in him. There is no principle binding each part of his life to every other, and holding the whole together. The other words by which we describe such a life all spring from the same conception. We call such a person dissolute; and dissolute means literally separated, loosed, broken apart. We call him dissipated; and dissipated means literally scattered, torn apart, thrown away.

These forms of statement all point to the same fact, that the unscrupulous pleasure-seeker, the selfish, vicious man has no consistent, continuous, coherent life whatever. "The unity of his being," as Janet says, "is lost in the multiplicity of his sensations." His life is a mere series of disconnected fragments. There is no growth, no development. There is nothing on which he can look with approval; no consistent career of devotion to worthy objective ends, the fruits of which can be witnessed in the improvement of the world in which he has lived, and stored up in the character which he has formed.

[194]

CHAPTER XXII.

God.

In the last chapter we saw that the particular objects and duties which make up our environment and moral life are not so many separate affairs; but all have a common relation to the self, and its realization. We saw that this common relation to the self gives unity to the world of objects, the life of duty, the nature of virtue, and the character which crowns right living.

There is, however, a deeper, more comprehensive unity in the moral world than that which each man constructs for his individual self. The world of objects is included in a universal order. The several duties are parts of a comprehensive righteousness, which includes the acts of all men within its rightful sway. The several virtues are so many aspects of one all-embracing moral ideal. The rewards and penalties which follow virtue and vice are the expression of a constitution of things which makes for righteousness. The Being whose thought includes all objects in one comprehensive universe of reason; whose will is uttered in the voice of duty; whose holiness is revealed in the highest ideal of virtue we can form; and whose authority is declared in those eternal and indissoluble bonds which bind [195]virtue and reward, vice and penalty, together, is God.

THE DUTY.

Communion with God is the safeguard of virtue, the secret of resistance to temptation, the source of moral and spiritual power.— Our minds are too small to carry consciously and in detail; our wills are too frail to hold in readiness at every moment the principles and motives of moral conduct. God alone is great enough for this.

We can make him the keeper of our moral precepts and the guardian of our lives. And then when we are in need of guidance, help, and strength, we can go to him, and by devoutly seeking to know and do his will, we can recover the principles and reinforce the motives of right conduct that we have intrusted to his keeping; and ofttimes we get, in addition, larger views of duty and nobler impulses to virtue than we have ever consciously possessed before. Just as the love of father or mother clarifies a child's perception of what is right, and intensifies his will to do it, so the love of God has power to make us strong to resist temptation, resolute to do our duty, and strenuous in the endeavor to advance the kingdom of righteousness and love.

Into the particular doctrines and institutions of religion it is not the purpose of this book to enter. These are matters which each individual learns best from his own father and mother, and from the church in which he has been brought up. Our [196]account of ethics, however, would be seriously incomplete, were we to omit to point out the immense and indispensable strength and help we may gain for the moral life, by approaching it in the religious spirit.

Ethics and religion each needs the other.—They are in reality, one the detailed and particular, the other the comprehensive and universal aspect of the same world of duty and virtue. Morality without religion is a cold, dry, dreary, mass of disconnected rules and requirements. Religion without morality, is an empty, formal, unsubstantial shadow. Only when the two are united, only when we bring to the particular duties of ethics the infinite aspiration and inspiration of religion, and give to the universal forms of religion the concrete contents of human and temporal relationships, do we gain a spiritual life which is at the same time clear and strong, elevated and practical, ideal and real.

THE VIRTUE.

Just as God includes all objects in his thought, all duties in his will, all virtues in his ideal; so the man who communes with him, and surrenders his will to him in obedience and trust and love, partakes of this same wholeness and holiness.—Loving God, he is led to love all that God loves, to love all good. And holiness is the love of all that is good and the hatred of all that is evil.

Complete holiness is not wrought out in its concrete relations all at once, nor ever in this earthly [197]life, by the religious, any more than by the moral man. Temptations are frequent all along the way, and the falls many and grievous to the last. But from all deliberately cherished identification of his inmost heart and will with evil, the truly religious man is forevermore set free. From the moment one's will is entirely surrendered to God, and the divine ideal of life and conduct is accepted, a new and holy life begins.

Old temptations may surprise him into unrighteous deeds; old habits may still assert themselves, old lusts may drift back on the returning tides of past associations; old vices may continue to crop out.

In reality, however, they are already dead. They are like the leaves that continue to look green upon the branches of a tree that has been cut down; or the momentum of a train after the steam is shut off and the brakes are on.

God, who is all-wise, sees that in such a man sin is in principle dead; and he judges him accordingly. If penitence for past sins and present falls be genuine; if the desire to do his will be earnest; He takes the will for the deed, penitence for performance, aspiration for attainment. Such judgment is not merely merciful. It is just. Or rather, it is the blending of mercy and justice in love. It is judgment according to the deeper, internal aspect of a man, instead of judgment according to the superficial, outward aspect. For the will is the center and core of personality. What a man desires and [198]strives for with all his heart, that he is. What he repents of and repudiates with the whole strength of his frail and imperfect nature, that he has ceased to be.

Thus religion, or whole-souled devotion to God, gives a sense of completeness, and attainment, and security, and peace, which mere ethics, or adjustment to the separate fragmentary objects which constitute our environment, can never give. The moral life is from its very nature partial, fragmentary, and finite. The religious life by penitence and faith and hope and love, rises above the finite with its limitations, and the temporal with its sins and failings, and lays hold on the infinite ideal and the eternal goodness, with its boundless horizon and its perfect peace. The religious life, like the moral, is progressive. But, as Principal Caird remarks, "It is progress, not towards, but within, the infinite." Union with God in sincere devotion to his holy will, is the "promise and potency" of harmonious relations with that whole ethical and spiritual universe which his thought and will includes.

THE REWARD.

The reward of communion with God and comprehensive righteousness of conduct is spiritual life.—The righteous man, the man who walks with God, is in principle and purpose identified with every just cause, with every step of human progress, with every sphere of man's well-being. To him property is a sacred trust, time a golden [199]opportunity, truth a divine revelation, Nature the visible garment of God, humanity a holy brotherhood, the family, society, and the state are God-ordained institutions, with God-given laws. Through the one fundamental devotion of his heart and will to God, the religious man is made a partaker in all these spheres of life in which the creative will of God is progressively revealed. All that is God's belong to the religious man. For he is God's child. And all these things are his inheritance.

To the religious man, therefore, there is open a boundless career for service, sacrifice, devotion and appropriation. Every power, every affection, every aspiration within him has its counterpart in the outward universe. The universe is his Father's house; and therefore his own home. All that it contains are so many opportunities for the development and realization of his God-given nature.

To dwell in active, friendly, loving relation to all that is without; to be

wedded to this goodly universeIn love and holy passion,

to be heirs with God of the spiritual riches it contains: this is life indeed. "The gift of God is eternal life."

Religion is the crown and consummation of ethics.—Religion gathers up into their unity the scattered fragments of duty and virtue which it has been the aim of our ethical studies to [200]discern apart. Religion presents as the will of the all-wise, all-loving Father, those duties and virtues which ethics presents as the conditions of our own self-realization. Religion is the perfect circle of which the moral virtues are the constituent arcs. Fullness of life is the reward of righteousness, the gift of God, the one comprehensive good, of which the several rewards which follow the practice of particular duties and virtues are the constituent elements.

THE TEMPTATION.

The universal will of God, working in conformity with impartial law, and seeking the equal good of all, often seems to be in sharp conflict with the interests of the individual self.—If his working is irresistible we are tempted to repine and rebel. If his will is simply declared, and left for us to carry out by the free obedience of our wills, then we are tempted to sacrifice the universal good to which the divine will points, and to assert instead some selfish interest of our own. Self-will is, from the religious point of view, the form of all temptation. The ends at which God aims when he bids us sacrifice our immediate private interests are so remote that they seem to us unreal; and often they are so vast that we fail to comprehend them at all. In such crises faith alone can save us—faith to believe that God is wiser than we are, faith to believe that his universal laws are better than any private exceptions we can make in our own interest, [201]faith to believe that the universal good is of more consequence than our individual gain. Such faith is hard to grasp and difficult to maintain; and consequently the temptation of self-will is exceedingly seductive, and is never far from any one of us.

THE VICE OF DEFECT.

Sin is short-coming, missing the mark of our true being, which is to be found only in union with God.—Sin is the attempt to live apart from God, or as if there were no God. It is transgression of his laws. It is the attempt to make a world of our own, from which in whole or in part we try to exclude God, and escape the jurisdiction of his laws. All wrong-doing, all vice, all neglect of duty, is in reality a violation of the divine will. But not until the individual comes to recognize the divine will, and in spite of this recognition that all duty is divine, deliberately turns aside from God and duty together, does vice become sin.

THE VICE OF EXCESS.

Devotion to God as distinct from or in opposition to devotion to those concrete duties and human relationship wherein the divine will is expressed, is hypocrisy.—"If a man say I love God and hateth his brother he is a liar: for he that loveth not his brother whom he hath seen, cannot love God whom he hath not seen."

Pure religion begins in faith and ends in works. It draws from God the inspiration to serve in [202]righteousness and love our fellow-men. If faith stop short of God, and rest in church, or creed, or priest; if work stop short of actual service of our fellow-men, and rest in splendor of ritual or glow of pious feeling, or orthodoxy of belief; then our religion becomes a vain and hollow thing, and we become Pharisees and hypocrites.

THE PENALTY.

The wages of sin is death.—The penalty of each particular vice we have seen to be the dwarfing, stunting, decay, and deadening of that particular side of our nature that is effected by it. Intemperance brings disease; wastefulness brings want; cruelty brings brutality; ugliness brings coarseness; exclusiveness brings isolation; treason brings anarchy. Just in so far as one cuts himself off from the moral order which is the expression of God's will; just in so far as there is sin, there is privation, deadening, and decay. As long as we live in this world it is impossible to live an utterly vicious life; to cut ourselves off completely from God and his order and his laws. To do that would be instant death. The man who should embody all the vices and none of the virtues, would be intolerable to others, unendurable even to himself. The penalty of an all-round life of vice and sin would be greater than man could endure and live. This fearful end is seldom reached in this life. Some redeeming virtues save even the worst of men from this full and final penalty of sin. The man, however, who deliberately [203]rejects God as his friend and guide to righteous living; the man who deliberately makes self-will and sin the ruling principle of his life, is started on a road, which, if followed to the end, leads inevitably to death. He is excluding himself from that sphere of good, that career of service and devotion, wherein alone true life is to be found. He is banishing himself to that outer darkness which is our figurative expression for the absence of all those rewards of virtue and the presence of all those penalties of vice which our previous studies have brought to our attention. "Sin, when it is full-grown, bringeth forth death." "The wages of sin is death."

THE END.

LA TOUR DU SILENCE

Pour Geneviève